I Heart Backpacking: How to Get Started

With 10 Easy to Moderate Trips in Oregon & Washington

BY LISA D. HOLMES & SARA CARROLL

© 2020 Lisa D. Holmes / Yulan Studio, Inc. No part of this publication may be reproduced or transmitted in any form or by any means, without permission in writing from the author.

Design, maps and photographs by Lisa D. Holmes (yulanstudio.com), unless otherwise indicated.

Maps utilize terrain map data by OpenStreetMap, under CC-BY-SA.

Published in Portland, Oregon, by Yulan Studio, Inc.

Printed in the United States.

First edition

ISBN 978-0-9915382-5-6

SAFETY NOTICE

This book is intended as a resource to help plan a backpacking trip. Although every attempt has been made to provide accurate and current information, the publisher and the authors are not responsible for any loss, damage or injury that may occur as a result of using this book – you hike at your own risk. Familiarize yourself with the area you intend to explore, check current weather reports, and contact the appropriate ranger station for more information on current conditions and regulations. You are responsible for your own safety and knowing your own limitations.

Contents

ABOUT THE AUTHORS — 4

WELCOME TO BACKPACKING — 6

BACKPACKING GEAR — 8
Backpacks — 10
Backpacking Tents — 12
Sleep Systems — 15
Kitchen Gear — 18
Water Treatment & Storage — 20
Clothing — 22
Footwear — 24
Toiletries — 25
Electronics — 26
Additional Gear — 27
The Ten Essentials — 28

SKILLS — 30
Trip Planning Basics — 31
Leave No Trace Seven Principles — 40
Physical Preparation — 42
Hiking Safety — 44
Trail Courtesies — 45
Navigation — 47
How to Pack a Backpack — 48
Basic First Aid — 50

Choosing a Campsite — 52
Camp Kitchens — 54
How to Hang a Food Bag — 55
Hydration & Filtering Water — 56
Food & Nutrition — 57
The Backcountry Bathroom — 58
Personal Hygiene — 59
Campfires — 60
Tips for Staying Warm — 61
Maintaining Your Gear — 62
Giving Forward — 63

BACKPACKING TRIPS — 64
Southwest Washington: Siouxon Creek — 66
Oregon Coast: Tillamook Head — 72
Columbia River Gorge: Wahtum Lake — 78
Eagle Cap Wilderness: Wallowas Lakes Basin — 84
Goat Rocks Wilderness: Snowgrass Flat — 90
Three Sisters Wilderness: Green Lakes — 96
Mount Adams Wilderness: Killen Creek — 102
Mount Hood Wilderness: Cairn Basin — 108
Mount Hood Wilderness: Burnt Lake — 114
Indian Heaven Wilderness: Deep Lake — 120

INDEX — 126

About the Authors

I'm a graphic designer and hiking book author based in Portland, Oregon. When I'm not designing websites and marketing materials for clients, I'm *diving deep* into the details of planning backpacking trips all over the beautiful Pacific Northwest. Learn more about my hiking books and follow my adventures at iheartpacificnorthwest.com.

Lisa "Deepdive" Holmes

My first backpacking trip was in April 2015. Up until that time, I'd only done day hikes and camped at established campgrounds. After moving to the Pacific Northwest, I fell in love with the whole outdoor experience, yet I used to say that I would never be a backpacker.

Why did I think this? For one, I thought it was beyond my hiking skill level. I had always been a slow hiker who didn't do big miles. Plus, I felt intimidated by the idea of sleeping in the wilderness. When I first started camping, it made me more at ease to know that there were other people close-by. I also didn't think that I'd be able to carry a fully loaded backpack across my living room, let alone up a mountain. And, let's face it, having to dig a hole to poop in was a bit of a deterrent as well. The rest of it – the hiking, the camping, the beautiful scenery – I knew that I liked that part already. I could barely get enough hiking in each year and was always ready to go.

But as I hiked more and more, I didn't always want to turn around and go back after reaching a day hike destination. I wanted time to linger. To get to know a place better. To truly feel the wilderness. I soon discovered that the best way to do this is to backpack. I'd been leading day hikes for women for a couple of years, and by doing so I got to know more and more women who backpacked. As I heard their stories – and was in awe of their experiences – I knew that this was something I wanted to do.

For my first trip, I chose to go to one of my favorite day hiking spots – Siouxon Creek in Southwest Washington (see the trip description on page 66). It's an easy hike that I had done several times, so it seemed like going to a place that is familiar would make it less intimidating. I talked a backpacking friend of mine into showing me the ropes, and off we went. I still remember feeling so proud every time a hiker passed us on the trail and acknowledged that we were going to spend the night there. I was a backpacker!

That trip proved to me that I could handle all of the things I thought I would struggle with, and not only could I handle it, I loved it. I was so happy to filter water for drinking. To cook my dinner on a backpacking stove! And to climb into my sleeping bag at the end of the day and feel like this is the best thing I've ever done. To sleep next to the never-ending sound of the creek, and to not be afraid. To wake up the next morning to the sound of birds chirping in the trees high above my head. Even digging a cathole became a point of pride for me. I'd done it. I'd conquered the thing I didn't think I could do. I was hooked. I was ready to go again. And again. And now I never want to stop. I just want to go farther and longer.

As I continue to backpack, I love the sense of empowerment that comes from being able to carry everything I need on my back in order to spend numerous days and nights in the wilderness. I feel stronger than I ever have, and I'm slowly increasing my capabilities one by one until I'm now capable of doing many things I never thought I would be able to do. I'm much more confident on the trail and in everyday life, thanks to backpacking!

Sara Carroll

I began backpacking late in my college years. Prior to that the only camping I'd done involved cars, flushing toilets, and electricity. It was akin to something the Griswald family might do in National Lampoon's Vacation. At that stage in my life, backpacking had never crossed my mind as something regular people did. In my mind, true wilderness exploration was left for the likes of John Muir and Ed Abbey.

That changed when I enrolled in college and saw that backpacking courses were offered through the university outdoor club. Up until that point, I had never slept in a tent smaller than 8ft x 6ft x 6ft. I'd never carried a pack bigger than my school bookbag. And it's probably safe to state that I'd never walked more than a couple miles at any one time. So, naturally, I signed up for the most difficult backpacking course I could find in the outdoor club's catalogue. The only prerequisite was that I could run a mile.

The course was a week-long expedition to the Boundary Waters of Northern Minnesota in early January. I borrowed or rented almost all of my gear as I didn't have any of my own. My snowshoes were wooden and had been used as decoration on a friend's wall. Purchased a pair of Korean War era military wool pants from the local surplus store for $10. I filled the rented pack until it was too heavy for me to lift on my own. And our group, led by a kind and knowledgeable University professor, headed out into a wintery environment that dipped well below -30 degrees and never got above 25 degrees. Suffice to say, it was mostly an uncomfortable week.

Despite the discomfort, extreme at times, it would be unfair to simply label the whole experience as uncomfortable. If that was the case I would never have signed up for the next trip to the Grand Canyon. I would never have become a backpacking guide. And I would never have completed the many, many trips over the years between that first trip and writing this book. Something has brought me back to the wilderness over and over again, and it isn't solely discomfort.

Each time I step into the backcountry I find there is beauty, exploration, self-efficacy, humbleness, and peace. And that is the short list! I have learned more about myself while wearing a backpack than I have in any facet of my life. Each ache I may feel as I climb switchbacks is a reminder of my strength. No doubt that as I climb those switchbacks, there is someone else who has not gotten off their couch that day. I may ache but I'm exploring! Like most backpackers, I will sometimes second guess my course and think that maybe I should have gone left at the fork rather than right. To use my skills and find reassurance in my path is empowering. The times where I am lucky enough to share laughter with friends while swimming in an alpine lake are moments of pure bliss. And I'm quieted each time I see a curious deer wander into camp. Backpacking brings about so many valuable moments. I choose to go on trail because of the richness these moments bring to my life.

I'm a believer that you have to work, at least a little, to experience some of life's greatest gifts. I have grown to understand that comfort is not the same as happiness. I backpack because there are very few things in life that bring me so much joy.

Over the past two decades, I've had the pleasure of backpacking in some of America's most spectacular wilderness areas. These experiences have allowed me to hone skills such as navigation, backcountry ethics, and primitive fire starting. I enjoy sharing this knowledge with others in the backpacking community. I currently reside in Utah's Wasatch Range with my supportive partner, Jason, and mountain-chihuahua, Louie.

Welcome to Backpacking

Whether you consider yourself a beginning backpacker, or it's been awhile since your last trip and you want to brush up on your skills, this book will help you to plan a trip, learn about gear options, and provide tips for the trip once you are on the trail and at camp.

The trip plans were chosen to showcase some of the best scenery in the Pacific Northwest, yet are easy to moderate trips that make it possible for a beginner to experience everything that backpacking has to offer.

This book focuses on low impact practices and encourages backpackers to be mindful stewards of the wilderness. It is our belief that we are all responsible for taking care of the places that we adventure in.

Backpacking Gear

For a current detailed list of recommended gear, see the **Backpacking Gear List** on the I Heart Pacific Northwest website: **iheartpacificnorthwest.com**

This guide will cover the basics on what to look for in backpacking gear but not make specific brand recommendations. The outdoor gear industry is ever-evolving, often with new models and high-tech and/or lighter weight options coming out on a regular basis.

"GEAR YOUR OWN GEAR"

Just like the saying "hike your own hike," when it comes to choosing your gear for backpacking, it's important to find what works for you based on your individual needs and preferences and not necessarily what your friends use or what is the most popular or award-winning.

Consider the trifecta of cost vs. weight vs. comfort and where your needs fall within each. For example, if carrying less weight matters, you may need to spend more on ultralight gear and forgo some comfort items. On the other hand, if comfort is king, your pack will most likely be heavier to carry. If you aren't in a position to invest a lot of money into backpacking gear, don't worry. It is possible to find bargains and/or buy used gear to get started. As you gain experience, you can slowly add or replace items if you choose to do so.

RENTING GEAR

Some gear retailers or university outdoor centers offer gear for rent at a reasonable cost. More experienced backpackers can be another valuable resource if they are willing to lend gear. In fact, it's recommended that new backpackers borrow or rent gear for their first few trips if they can. Renting or borrowing gear not only makes backpacking accessible in terms of cost but it also gives a novice backpacker an opportunity to try out different styles of gear before investing in it.

LIGHTWEIGHT BACKPACKING

Almost all backpackers wish they had focused more on the weight of each item when initially purchasing gear. It doesn't take long to realize that carrying less weight in your pack has great benefits. It's less stressful on your body and makes it easier to cover more miles or hike in difficult terrain with less weight on your back. It also doesn't zap your energy like carrying a heavy load does.

While what each person can carry varies based on their overall body type and size, age and physical strength, a general rule is to carry no more than 25% of your body weight.

The best way to lighten your load is to take less gear. It's easy to get in the "just in case" mentality, especially when it comes to safety and comfort. You can likely get by with less than you think. Each time you go on a backpacking trip, make note of items that don't get used. Also think about how to get multiple uses out of your gear. For example, a headlamp can provide enough light in your tent at night so you don't need to bring a separate lantern. A cookpot can be used as a mug instead of bringing a separate mug.

Key items to consider for lightweight gear are the largest and heaviest items needed: a backpack, shelter, sleeping bag and pad. Choose the backpack last since the fit and comfort will be largely based on the gear that goes in it. Keep in mind that carrying less weight won't matter if the backpack you choose rubs you the wrong way (literally) when it's fully loaded.

It can be helpful to weigh all of your gear and make note of your base weight – everything except food, water and fuel. A kitchen scale works well for smaller gear, and a luggage scale is useful for weighing a fully loaded pack.

When considering how lightweight to go, continue to keep safety in mind. Being strategic about pack weight does not mean taking unnecessary risks. You'll still need to take the essentials with you.

PRACTICE USING NEW GEAR

Once you've obtained gear, take the time to familiarize yourself with it before leaving home. Set up your tent, inflate your sleeping pad and try out your stove prior to getting on the trail. It can be very frustrating to get to camp and realize that you do not know how to use your gear or are missing important items.

Backpacks on display at Next Adventure in Portland, Oregon

Backpacks

A backpack will be one of the most important purchases you make since it is what you use to carry all of your gear, ideally in well-balanced comfort. There are many choices in pack styles, sizes, shapes and features, so take the time to find the right one for you and your gear.

FRAME STYLES

Backpack frames come in three types: internal, external, and frameless. Internal frame packs are the most readily available and common choice for the average backpacker. These packs are built to evenly balance loads and stabilize weight. External frame packs, while still produced, have for the most part gone the way of the dinosaur. Most people using an external frame pack are doing so in order to haul heavy specialty equipment such as inflatable rafts. The frameless pack is most utilized by the ultralight community. The lack of frame in this pack style allows for a significant weight savings, but frameless packs are typically not advised for carrying over 25 pounds.

CAPACITY

A common question that a new backpacker has when purchasing a backpack is, "which capacity do I need?" The answer to that question will depend upon the typical length of your trips and the type of gear you plan to carry. It's a good idea to purchase most of your backpacking gear before considering a backpack since you'll need to find one that fits what you plan to take.

For most people getting started, a backpack between 50-65 liters is recommended. If you have ultralight gear, you may be able to use a 40-50 liter or smaller backpack. Keep in mind that having a pack that has extra room doesn't mean that you have to fill it to capacity, but a pack that's too small for your gear can't be expanded.

FITTING

When it comes to choosing a specific backpack, it is highly recommended to go to a retailer to get fitted (ask for assistance with this) and try on multiple packs prior to purchase. Most backpacks are available in sizes that can range from extra small to large. The size is determined by torso length, not overall body size. When shopping for a pack, add weight to allow you to test it loaded. Most retailers have weighted items for this use. A loaded pack feels completely different than an empty one, and will change how it fits you.

Women-specific backpacks are made a bit differently than unisex backpacks, with a narrower and shorter torso, and a contoured shape in the hip belt and shoulder straps to fit the female build. Some women's packs also have more padding in the hip belt and shoulders.

BACKPACK FEATURES

Pack access: most backpacks have top loader access for placing items into the main compartment of the pack through a top opening. Some offer front or side zippers for additional access to the main panel.

Ventilation: to help prevent your back from getting sweaty or overheated, some packs have a raised mesh back panel that is contoured away from your body, or a "chimney" section on the back panel to improve airflow.

Sleeping bag panel: a zippered compartment at the bottom of a pack for storing a sleeping bag.

Top lid: provides extra storage capacity with a "lid" that sits on top of the main compartment. Top lids can be useful for carrying small items that you need frequent access to. Some can be detached and used as a day pack.

Shoulder straps: choose a pack with shoulder straps that are well padded, easily adjustable, and contoured to fit the shape of your body.

Hip belts: Since the weight of a pack rests on the hips, a well-fitted and padded hip belt is crucial to comfortable backpacking.

Hip belt pockets: one of the most useful features on a backpack are hip belt pockets – used for storing small items for easy access while hiking.

Load lifters: located at the top of the shoulder straps and connected to the top of the pack frame, load lifters are used to keep the top of your pack from pulling away from your body.

Sternum strap: attaches across your mid-chest to connect the shoulder straps and prevent your pack from shifting while hiking. Often, the attachment buckle on a sternum strap will have a built-in whistle, perfect for reaching in an emergency situation.

Compression straps: located on the sides of a pack, compression straps are used to bring a load closer to the pack frame and can be used to secure gear on the outside of a pack.

Hydration sleeve: for carrying water reservoirs, often in a pocket that separates it from the main compartment.

Pockets: the number of pockets on a pack varies greatly. Some offer multiple external pockets with zippered access for additional gear storage and organization. Stretchy side pockets are common on most packs, handy for holding water bottles, tent poles, and other items that don't fit as well inside a pack. A large front mesh pocket is useful for stashing wet gear.

Shoulder strap pouch: while not included on most backpacks, you may consider purchasing a pouch that attaches to the shoulder straps for holding items that don't fit in hip belt pockets, for example: a smartphone, sunglasses, or a compass.

External straps: on the outside bottom of a pack, useful for attaching bulky items like sleeping pads or tents.

Additional attachments: loops and tie-outs for attaching trekking poles, ice axes and/or rope.

RAIN PROTECTION

Very few backpacks are completely waterproof, so to protect the gear inside your backpack from getting wet, invest in a pack cover and/or use a heavy duty plastic bag to line the inside of your pack. A trash compactor bag works well for a liner since it is more durable than typical garbage bags and can stand up to being repeatedly stuffed with gear.

For extra protection, especially if there is rain in the forecast, you may want to store your sleeping bag, clothing, and electronics in waterproof stuff sacks.

> For info on loading a backpack with gear, see **How to Pack a Backpack** on page 48.

Tent selection at Next Adventure in Portland, Oregon

Backpacking Tents

The ideal backpacking tent will have the combination of features, weight, comfort, and durability for the type of trips you plan to do. Of course, cost is also an important factor. A high quality tent can be quite expensive, so it's good to know what to look for before making an investment in your shelter.

The least expensive tents are usually intended for car camping, often weighing over 5 pounds or more depending on the size of the tent. It is possible to purchase a tent that will work for both car camping and backpacking, but for the purpose of this book, we'll cover what to look for in backpacking tents.

TYPES OF TENTS

DOUBLE-WALL TENTS

The double-wall tent is the most utilized type, with a mesh inner tent and a separate rainfly that covers it and provides weather protection. These tents work well to keep water from the outside out, while allowing moisture and condensation from the inside to escape. They also provide flexible set up options, including the removal of the rainfly in good weather. Some offer a "fast-pitch" option, utilizing the rainfly with a footprint and leaving out the inner tent for a lighter option.

SINGLE-WALL TENTS

Single-wall tents can be advantageous to those wanting to cut down on pack weight. These tents are made of a combination of fabric and mesh and do not have the rainfly and internal walls as separate pieces. While all tents can experience condensation build-up on the inside of the walls, it's more apparent with a single-wall tent since there's only one layer of material. Careful site selection and set up can help to alleviate condensation by allowing greater air flow.

THREE-SEASON & FOUR-SEASON TENTS

The vast majority of tents are made for three-season use in the spring, summer and fall. Four-season tents are designed for use in harsher conditions, with sturdier construction to withstand high wind and snow loads. They tend to be a lot heavier, with more fabric coverage, less mesh and bulkier poles.

TENT SPECIFICATIONS

WEIGHT

A tent is one of the main gear items that comprise your backpacking base weight, so it's important to use weight as one of the most important criteria when purchasing a tent. However, consider the type of trips you plan to do before going for the lowest possible weight tent. For example, if you plan to cover a lot of miles on backpacking trips, an ultralight tent will make a big difference in the overall comfort of your hike. On the other hand, if you plan to hike shorter miles or set up a basecamp and day hike from there, a tent with additional features and roominess that weighs slightly more might be a better option.

The specs for a tent usually list the trail weight (sometimes labeled as the minimum weight) and the packaged weight. Trail weight is typically only the tent body, rainfly and poles. The packaged weight is everything that comes packaged with the tent, including the tent body, rainfly, poles, stakes, and any guylines, stuff sacks, repair kits or instructions that may be included. The actual weight that you carry will vary based on the parts of the tent you choose to take on each trip. The packaged weight will generally come closer to what you'll carry versus the trail weight.

In general, a lightweight backpacking tent should weigh about 2 to 2.5 pounds per person, while ultralight tents will be closer to 1 to 1.5 pounds per person. When sharing a tent it is possible to split the weight by having one person carry the tent body and poles, and the other carry the rainfly, guylines, and stakes.

CAPACITY

Tents are sold in one, two or three person sizes, although there is no industry standard for these designations so you'll need to compare each tent's measurements in order to find what works for you. Most backpacking tents tend to be a snug fit, so if you need a bit of extra space to spread out or to store gear, consider sizing up.

PACKABILITY

Tent specs include the packed size, which will help you determine how well it fits in a backpack or if it will need to be attached to the outside.

FABRICS

The majority of tents available are made of nylon or polyester fabric with a polyurethane (PU) waterproof coating on the inside of the rainfly and a DWR or silicone coating on the outside to repel rain. These coatings can wear off over time due to sun exposure and abrasion and may need to be reapplied. The weight of the fabric is designated as denier, with most tents utilizing 30-70 denier. Lightweight and ultralight tents typically use 15 denier or lighter fabric which can be less durable.

Silnylon is a material with the silicone embedded in the nylon, making it stronger, lighter weight, and more waterproof than coated fabrics. The fabric has a silky feel that is slippery. Since seam tape won't stick to silnylon, seams must be sealed with a liquid sealant. Some tents come with this applied during the manufacturing process, but for those that aren't, it can be done at home with silicone and a foam brush.

Dyneema (formerly called Cuban Fiber) is the lightest fabric option currently available. It's completely waterproof without the need for coatings. It's also the most expensive and currently not in use by most major tent manufacturers. However, there are many cottage-industry gear manufacturers offering ultralight tents utilizing Dyneema fabric. It used to be that ultralight tents had much smaller interiors, but with the use of fabrics such as Dyneema, an ultralight tent can be spacious and weigh much less than a comparable traditional tent.

TENT FEATURES

ROOMINESS

To determine the overall roominess of a tent, look at the square footage, height, length and width. Tents with vertical walls will be much roomier than those with sloping walls. This is often achieved with the addition of short poles that extend across the width of the tent to pull the walls out wider. Also consider the size of the vestibules for storing gear, freeing up space inside.

For taller people, pay attention to the tent length and height to make sure there's enough space to keep a sleeping bag from touching the ends when laying down, and enough head space for sitting up without hitting the top of the tent.

It may seem like a good idea to get a larger shelter that will accommodate more people and a lot of gear, but larger tents are heavier and can make it difficult to find a campsite that will fit the larger footprint. Additionally, if there's a lot of empty space, it will tend to be colder than a smaller tent with less air to warm.

DOORS AND VESTIBULES

The placement of the entry to a tent can have a big impact on ease of use and comfort. Some of the lightest tents available use a single front entry, while side entry tents are much easier to enter/exit without contorting and twisting around to get in and out. This is especially important in a two-person tent, where having two doors is advantageous not only to prevent crawling over your tent mate, but also for the extra space an additional vestibule provides. Vestibules are the space outside of the tent door, sheltered by the rainfly. They provide an area to store gear, clean muddy items, or change out of wet clothing prior to entering the main tent area.

TENT POLES

Most tents utilize dedicated aluminum or carbon fiber poles for supporting the structure. In a hubbed design, multiple poles are combined and use a hub, shaped like a spoke, with poles coming off of each point.

Instead of dedicated poles, some ultralight tents rely on the use of trekking poles. An advantage to using trekking poles is if you already use them for hiking, the weight of dedicated poles is saved. However, if you want to use your trekking poles for hiking while your tent is set up, you'll need to remove them from the tent and/or bring a dedicated pole for your tent.

TENT STAKES

Stakes are used to secure a tent to the ground, to help provide a taut set up, and to prevent the rainfly from touching the sides of the tent. Each tent varies on the number of stakes needed for proper set up, and not all tents come with the number of stakes needed, so check to make sure you have enough stakes before using your tent on a backpacking trip. Most of the stakes that ship with tents aren't the best quality. Consider upgrading to sturdier versions, such as a Y stake with fins that have great holding power in hard or rocky soil.

VENTS

To prevent condensation build up on the inside of a tent, vents are used to allow moist air to escape. High quality tents offer multiple ways to vent, with strategic placement of the vents for cross ventilation. Additionally, tents with two doors will allow air to flow through the space when the vestibules are opened.

WEATHER PROTECTION

For extra protection from rain and wind, look for a rainfly that extends low to the ground. Additionally, tents with a bathtub floor (fabric that extends up the tent walls a few inches) will help to prevent moisture and cold air from entering the tent.

FOOTPRINTS

The use of a footprint is optional, but can help protect the floor of a tent from abrasion and punctures and prolong its life. Many tent manufacturers offer footprints that are sold separately for each model of tent they sell. For a lightweight and less expensive option, materials such as Polycro (the same material used for sealing windows) and Tyvek (used in the construction of homes) can be trimmed to the size of your tent. Footprints should be slightly smaller than the floor of a tent to prevent water from pooling underneath it.

ADDITIONAL FEATURES

There are a number of options that may be offered in a tent, including multiple pockets or even built-in lighting. Pockets are useful for storing smaller items for easy access, such as a headlamp or eyeglasses. Most models have at least one loop on the interior, useful for hanging a light, or with multiple loops, a gear loft can be attached to keep lightweight gear off the tent floor. Loops can also be used to attach a line for hanging items to dry during inclement weather.

OTHER SHELTER OPTIONS

Additional options for backpacking shelters include tarps, bivys and hammocks.

Tarps are a single piece of material that is set up using guy lines and/or poles and do not offer any mesh for bug protection. They are one of the lightest weight options for those who don't need full coverage, but they require more skill in order to set up properly.

Bivys are intended to provide weather protection in a space not much larger than a sleeping bag, acting as a slipcover over the bag. Due to their small size, they can feel claustrophobic and don't provide storage for gear.

Hammocks are increasingly used for backpacking, with options for rainflies, mesh for bug protection, and underquilts for warmth. Of course, hammocks rely on having trees suitable for hanging, so they must be used in areas that can accommodate them.

WHERE TO PURCHASE

Outdoor retailers typically carry double-wall, 3-season tents by manufacturers such as Big Agnes, North Face, Kelty, Marmot, MSR, Nemo, and Sierra Designs. In addition, some retailers like REI offer their own brand of tents.

Also consider purchasing gear from one of the smaller cottage-industry companies such as TarpTent, Zpacks, Six Moon Designs, or Gossamer Gear. These companies focus on ultralight gear and offer single-wall and double-wall tents, many of which are made in the U.S. While you may be able to find products from these companies at smaller local retailers, most of these products will need to be purchased directly from the companies who make them.

Sleep Systems

Sleeping bags at Next Adventure in Portland, Oregon

A sleep system for backpacking includes a sleeping bag or quilt, a sleeping pad, and a pillow if you prefer to use one. Everyone's needs for warmth and comfort are different, so it's important to find the right combination of these items that works for you to prevent sleepless nights.

Pay special attention to the weight of each item when making a purchase since the combined weight of your sleep system will have a big impact your overall pack weight. Packability is an important factor as well, since the amount of space your sleep system takes in your pack will impact the capacity of your backpack.

SLEEPING BAGS AND QUILTS

INSULATION TYPE

Down sleeping bags use duck or goose down for insulation. They tend to be warmer, lighter weight, more compressible, and have better longevity than synthetic-filled bags. While down loses insulating abilities when wet, most sleeping bags currently available utilize down that's been treated with a hydrophobic coating to make it water resistant. The Responsible Down Standard (RDS) is a certification program to ensure that down comes from ducks and geese that have been treated well and are not force fed or live-plucked.

Synthetic sleeping bags are filled with polyester for insulation. They are less expensive than down and they dry faster and retain insulating abilities better when wet. And for those with allergies, synthetic fill is non-allergenic. However, they are much heavier and bulkier than down sleeping bags, and they tend to lose their insulating properties after several years of use.

TEMPERATURE RATING

The temperature rating on a sleeping bag is based on the lowest temperature at which the bag will keep an "average sleeper" warm. Most sleeping bag manufacturers use either the EN (European Norm) rating system or the newer ISO rating system for determining the temperature range a bag is suited for. While these ratings are accepted as the most dependable standards available, all ratings are subjective and don't take into account individual body types. Two additional factors that greatly influence sleeping bag warmth are: 1) your sleeping pad's insulation value, and 2) how well the shape of the sleeping bag fits your body.

Warm sleepers may be fine in temperatures a bag is rated for, but most people tend to stay warmer in bags that are rated 10-20 degrees lower than the temps they will be camping in. As a rule of thumb, women tend to be cold sleepers and may do better with a women's bag. Bags made for women often have a wider hip area, narrower shoulders, and additional insulation in the footbox and torso.

SIZE AND SHAPE

Sleeping bags and quilts work by using your body heat to warm the air pockets trapped around you, so finding one that fits the shape of your body will help to keep you warmer. To accommodate various body types and heights, bags are available in several different lengths and shapes.

Mummy-shaped bags are the most common and traditional style, offering the highest warmth-to-weight ratio due to their trim shape. Some are more constricting than others, so compare the specs for length, shoulder girth, hip gerth, and footbox width to find one that works for you.

Rectangular, semi-rectangular, and spoon-shaped bags offer more wiggle room for those that find mummy bags too restrictive. Keep in mind, however, that the more room you have in the sleeping bag, the harder your body has to work to stay warm, so don't get a bag that is much larger than you need.

Trying out sleeping bags at outdoor retailers is a good way to find the shape and size that you need. When possible, try it out on a sleeping pad similar to one that you'll use with the bag.

mummy-style sleeping bags with hoods

backpacking quilt

BACKPACKING QUILTS

Backpacking quilts are popular with ultralight backpackers, especially since they are generally 20-30% lighter in weight than sleeping bags. They don't have hoods and are made to go over your top and sides but not underneath, saving extra material and insulation over bags that are fully enclosed with zippers.

Quilts offer more flexibility than sleeping bags in terms of how they are used. Some can be fully opened and used like a comforter in warmer weather, and then closed to make more of a mummy bag shape when it's colder. They often include straps for attaching to a sleeping pad to allow for flexibility in how tight or loose you prefer it to be, and allow for easier movement while sleeping.

FEATURES

Hoods: sleeping bags with hoods help to keep your head warm, and most are adjustable so you can cinch it around your face in colder conditions. For bags or quilts without a hood, wear a hat to keep your head warm overnight.

Draft collars: located at the top of the sleeping bag, a draft collar is an extra piece of insulation that prevents warm air from escaping and cold air from entering the bag.

Zippers: the length of a zipper varies on sleeping bags, some include baffles alongside the zipper to prevent drafts.

Pockets: some bags include small pockets useful for stashing smaller items like eyeglasses or headlamps.

Pad loops or sleeves: some bags have sleeves or loops for attaching to your sleeping pad. This is helpful to prevent sliding around on the pad.

Liners: sleeping bag liners are used to add warmth and keep your sleeping bag clean. Another option is bring additional

air mattress sleeping pad

layers to wear while sleeping, saving the weight and cost of an additional item in your set up.

Stuff sacks and storage: to prolong the life of a sleeping bag or quilt, it should be stored uncompressed whenever not in use. Compression sacks can be useful for fitting a bag into a backpack, but use of a larger breathable stuff sack is much better for long-term storage.

SLEEPING PADS

The purpose of a sleeping pad is to insulate you from the ground and provide comfort for a good night's sleep.

TYPES OF PADS

Closed-cell foam pads are the most basic starting point for sleeping pads. These pads are made of dense foam with tiny air pockets and are the most affordable option on the market. They come in styles that either roll up or fold like an accordion. While you'll never have to worry about puncturing a foam pad, they don't offer much comfort and are bulky to carry.

Self-inflating pads use a mixture of open-cell foam and air and employ a valve system to automatically fill the pad. Many backpackers like this option because they provide more cushion than closed-cell foam pads, and are more durable than air pads. Some of the best insulation can be found in this group of pads. However, they tend to be heavy and usually need to be carried on the outside of a backpack due to their bulkiness.

Air pads are a popular choice for backpacking, providing more loft for comfort than any other pad type and compressing to a much smaller size for packing. There are many styles of air pads available, including those with insulation or reflective layers for extra warmth, and the shapes vary from rectangular to mummy-style for less added weight. They need to be inflated by blowing into them, although some models come with a built-in pump or a pump sack. Be sure to check the style of valve used so the pump sack matches the pad valve. Because these pads are made of technical material with innovative insulation, they are currently the most expensive option on the market. It's a good idea to carry a repair kit in case they get punctured and leak. The fabric used on some pads can make a crinkly sound, so if that will bother you (or your campmates), try one out at an outdoor retailer before purchasing.

WARMTH RATING

The R-value or temperature range for a sleeping pad rates how well it insulates the body from the ground. R-values range from 1 to 10, with higher numbers providing the most insulation. For typical summer sleeping, an R-value of around 3 is desirable. For colder conditions, a rating of 5 or higher is recommended. And when the temps dip extra low, consider adding a closed-cell foam pad under a self-inflating or air pad.

PILLOWS

Not everyone needs a pillow for a good night's sleep, but many people do. A pillow can be as simple as a stuff sack with clothing or a puffy jacket inserted. While this method doesn't provide much loft, it does use what you already have so is a lightweight option. If you need more support in a pillow, there are many types available, including air pillows, foam pillows, and down pillows. Foam pillows tend to be heavier and take up more space in your pack but are often the most like a pillow from home, while air pillows tend to be the lightest option. Fine-tune the softness or hardness of an air pillow by adjusting the amount of air inside. They are often more comfortable when not fully filled.

compressible foam pillow

Kitchen Gear

Choosing your kitchen gear for backpacking should be based on how you plan to cook and eat meals on trips. For a lot of backpackers, the need to boil water to pour into a prepackaged freeze-dried meal and to make instant coffee or tea is all they need. For others, it can be more elaborate, with a stove and cookset tailored to their cooking style.

BACKPACKING STOVES

When choosing a stove think about how you will use it most. Will you just be boiling water or do you want a simmer feature for cooking in a pot? Will you need the stove to work flawlessly at high elevations or during winter camping trips? Or will you eventually find yourself backpacking in areas of the world where certain types of fuel may not be found? There is no one stove that will fit every person's needs but this guide may help you find the features you require.

There are four main types of stoves to consider for backpacking use: canister, integrated canister, liquid fuel, and alternative fuel.

Canister stoves are are the most popular choice for most backpackers due to being small, lightweight and easy to use. These stoves have been designed to take up minimal space, with pot supports that fold down when not in use. Canister stoves run off of a pressurized blend of propane and butane or isobutane fuel, available at outdoor retailers. Connect the stove to the fuel canister via a threaded valve, then set your pot on top of the stove supports. To light, use a lighter or look for a stove with a built-in piezo igniter. Models with this feature are lit by turning on the fuel, then press the piezo button which creates a spark to light the stove. Burner heads on canister stoves vary in size and style. Some offer larger burners that work well for group cooking, while compact burners generally perform better with smaller lightweight pots. The shape of the burner head affects performance as well. For example, concave burner heads provide better wind resistance.

Integrated canister stoves feature a burner that connects to a pot with heat exchangers on the bottom. The heat exchanger makes integrated canister stoves more fuel efficient and wind resistant than regular canister stoves. Though they tend to be a bit heavier and bulkier, they are popular due to being the easiest to use of all types of backpacking stoves. Some models are meant for boiling water only, while other models feature the ability to control the temperature for simmering capability.

Remote canister stoves have a fuel hose to separate the burner from the fuel canister. These stoves often have a larger and more stable base to set pots on, and the ability to invert the fuel canister makes this type of stove perform better than other canister stoves in freezing or below freezing temps.

> *Tip: when empty, you can recycle fuel canisters by puncturing them. Make sure they are empty first, and use a crunch tool to make the job easier.*

Liquid gas stoves, like remote canister stoves, separate the burner from the fuel source, connecting to a bottle filled with liquid gas. The fuel is usually inexpensive white gas, though some models will also work with diesel, kerosene, or auto fuel. The liquid fuel stove requires more effort to use since they need to be primed before use and require regular cleaning and maintenance. In return for the added work, these stoves will perform in extremely cold temperatures and at higher elevations.

Alternative fuel stoves include alcohol stoves, solid fuel stoves, and wood burning stoves. Alcohol stoves are especially liked by thru-hikers since they are ultralight and don't rely on purchasing fuel canisters. They run on denatured alcohol which is readily available and inexpensive. There are even DIY options for making your own stove using a soda or cat food can. Solid fuel stoves are similar to alcohol stoves except they utilize fuel tablets. They are also ultralight, but the fuel has an odor that can be offensive to some, and it leaves a sticky residue on your pot. A downside to both of these stoves is that they don't burn as hot and can take a long time to boil water. During high fire danger times, using them may be prohibited since they don't have a way to turn them off.

Wood burning stoves are another alternative fuel option to consider. Modern wood burning systems are efficient, lightweight, and some even generate enough electricity to charge electronic gadgets. Wood burning stoves need dry fuel (and plenty of it) to work. They also may be prohibited during periods of high fire danger.

COOKWARE & UTENSILS

Unless you plan to do gourmet cooking, you probably only need to add a cook pot, mug and a spoon or spork to your cookset. For the best packability, look for items that can nest inside your cook pot. A small cookpot with folding handles can work well as a mug, with the benefit of being able to heat water directly in the pot. For utensils, consider a longer handle for stirring (and keeping your hand out of the heat) while cooking, or for easier access when eating directly from a food package. Spoons with silicone coatings on the edges can make getting every last bit of food left in a cookpot or package much easier.

FOOD STORAGE

Proper storage of food while backpacking is critical, not only for protecting your food, but also to make sure that wildlife doesn't become accustomed to looking for food from humans. Plan to store your food at least 100 feet from camp. There are three main options for food storage in the backcountry: food sacks, bear bags, and bear canisters.

food storage options

Food sacks, which need to be properly hung for food storage while backpacking, can be any type of bag that can hold your food and be fastened shut. A waterproof dry sack is a good option. Food sack kits are often sold with a carabiner and a small "rock" sack for throwing rope over a high branch.

Bear bags are made from a sturdy specialty fabric that bears can't tear into. They are a good option where bear canisters are not required. Instead of needing to hang high like a food sack, they can be tied around a tree or branch. There are several models available: bear-resistant, rodent-resistant, and a model that combines both types of material into one bag.

Odor-proof plastic bags are recommended for use in both food sacks and bear bags.

Bear canisters are hard-sided containers made from plastic or carbon fiber with lids that wildlife cannot open. They are the heaviest food storage option available, but they are also the easist to store and the most effective at keeping all types of wildlife from getting into your food. They are sold in various sizes so you can choose one based on the capacity needed.

Since you'll also need to store all scented items in your food bag or bear canister, make sure to purchase one large enough to hold everything.

For info on camp kitchen setup, food preparation, cleanup, and how to hang a food sack, see **Camp Kitchen** on page 54.

Water Treatment & Storage

Plan to treat water with either chemicals, purifiers, or a filter any time that it will be collected from natural sources such as rivers, streams, lakes, or snowmelt.

FILTERS AND PURIFIERS

The difference between a purifier and filter comes down to the type of microorganisms being removed from water. Generally speaking, water filters will remove most microorganisms found in the United States, including bacteria and protoza. Purifiers go one step further by removing viruses from water, which can be helpful in developing countries.

WATER TREATMENT OPTIONS

Filters and purifiers are available in many different styles, including pumps, gravity systems, straws, squeeze bags, bottles, UV lights, and more. Each system has its own merits but the most common methods used by backpackers are squeeze filters, gravity systems, and chemicals.

Squeeze filters are a popular option due to being lightweight, inexpensive and easy to use. Fill a hydration pouch, bladder or bag with water, then squeeze the water through the filter into a clean container. Look for filters with a high flow rate and small pore size for the best performance. Bottle filters and straw filters work much the same as squeeze filters but tend to be better for on-the-go needs rather than for filtering larger quantities of water.

filtering water using gravity

Gravity systems are a great option for basecamps and groups since they allow you to quickly filter a large quantity of water. With a gravity system, collect water in a "dirty" container or bag, then connect it and the filter to a "clean" water container. Hang or hold the water you collected higher than the clean water container to allow gravity to do the work. Most systems use hydration bladder-type bags and hoses for water collection and storage, but options exist for connecting filters to water bottles as well.

Chemical treatment is one of the lightest and easiest options available but it takes more time to be effective. Just add iodine or chlorine-based tablets or drops to water and wait — anywhere from 30 minutes to 4 hours. Chemicals treat bacteria, viruses and protozoans, but they don't remove particulates so the use of a pre-filter (such as a bandana) is recommended. Some people don't like the off-flavor of chemically-treated water.

water filtering and hydration system

filtering water using a pump with a pre-filter

Pumps (available as both filters and purifiers) are especially useful when the water is shallow or difficult to access. Hold the device in your hand, place the hose (and pre-filter if included) into the water source, then pump to pull the water through the filter. Pumps tend to be a bit bulky and heavy compared to other types of filters, often need maintenance, and they can be tedious to use, especially after a long day of hiking.

UV lights purify water using ultraviolet light to sterilize pathogens, bacteria and viruses. They are simple to use and provide filtered water fast, but they tend to be expensive and require batteries to operate. UV lights work best in clear water. Plan to use a pre-filter if the water source is cloudy, murky or filled with sediment.

Boiling water to purify it is also an option for backpackers. Bringing water to a rolling boil will wipe out all harmful microorganisms and is a good backup system in case your filter breaks (or gets lost). The disadvantage of this technique is that boiling and subsequently cooling water takes more time and will use additional fuel.

WATER STORAGE

While backpacking, you'll need a way to collect and store the filtered water that you'll use for drinking, cooking, and cleaning.

Water bottles have traditionally been the best option for drinking water while hiking, but unless you have easy access to your water bottle while hiking, you may not stay hydrated as well as you could. If using a water bottle as your main source for hydration while hiking, look for a backpack with stretchy mesh side pockets that allow you to reach water bottles without removing the pack. Hard-sided water bottles are the most durable but also heavier and bulkier than a soft water bottle that can be folded up for stowing when not using.

Hydration bladders hold 1-3 liters of water and make it easier to stay hydrated while hiking by taking sips from a hose that attaches to the bladder. They can also be good for storing filtered water at camp so you have plenty to cook and clean with. Using adapter kits that work with filters, you can set up an in-line filter or gravity setup for filling your bladder with filtered water.

Go ultralight: many long distance hikers use disposable plastic water bottles for their water storage. This option is popular for its weight savings (a typical one-liter bottle weighs about one ounce) and can be picked up at most grocers or convenience stores. Choose a rigid-type plastic bottle for better durabilty. Carry several and combine with a squeeze filter and a lightweight bladder for collecting water and you'll have a full water storage and filtering system that weighs far less than other options.

For info on hydration and filtering water, see **Hydration & Filtering Water** on page 56.

Clothing

A common mistake that backpackers make is either bringing too much clothing or bringing clothing that is inappropriate for the conditions. Learn how to use layers to stay warm and dry while taking fewer items.

FABRIC TYPES

When choosing clothing for hiking and backpacking, avoid cotton. When cotton gets wet, either from precipitation or from your body sweat, it doesn't wick the moisture away and takes a long time to dry. This can lead to losing body heat and increasing the risk of hypothermia. Wool and synthetic materials that wick moisture away from the body while retaining body heat are a much better choice.

Wool, once hated for its itchy character, has been revived by the merino wool industry. This type of wool is softer and much less itchy. Wool has natural wicking properties, insulates well, and dries relatively quickly. It also doesn't hold onto body odors as much as other fabric types. While it does tend to be more expensive, wool is available in varying thicknesses to suit differing needs.

Synthetic materials include nylon and polyester. Synthetics are excellent at moisture wicking, quick drying, durable, and they tend to be less expensive. A downside is that they have a tendency to hold odors more than natural fibers.

Silk is a softer and lighter material that isn't used as often for outdoor clothing. It tends to be a weaker fabric that snags easily and has a tendency to hold body odor.

HOW MUCH TO BRING?

For most three-season backpacking, you may only need one set of clothes for hiking, one set of base layers for sleeping, several pairs of socks and an extra pair of underwear. In colder weather, bring an extra layer to stay warm and dry, such as a lightweight fleece top or pants. These items can also be worn with base layers for sleeping. Instead of bringing a change of clothes for each day, consider doing laundry at camp. Simply fill a plastic bag with water and swish the clothes around, then wring out and hang on a tree, rock, or the back of your pack to dry.

LAYERING

Layering allows you to adjust your wardrobe for anything nature throws your way, plus it captures pockets of air between the layers which add warmth in cool weather.

Wearing multiple lightweight layers is better than fewer bulkier layers. Not only will this allow you to make more adjustments, lightweight items will fit in your pack better than bulky items. For example, a long sleeve shirt topped by a lightweight fleece or puffy and a rain jacket provides more options for adjustability than a heavy shirt and a bulky insulated waterproof jacket.

Base layers

Base layers are for moisture management. A next-to-skin layer, they work by wicking moisture away from your skin and can also help to prevent chafing. In cooler weather, long underwear-style base layers keep you warm and dry. In warmer weather, base layers can prevent sweat from making you feel sticky and clammy. Examples of base layers include underwear, bras, socks, long or short sleeve tops, and pants, skirts, or shorts.

Bring a separate pair of base layers and socks just for sleeping. Not only will doing so keep your sleeping bag cleaner, it will also prevent body oils and dirt from affecting the loft and warmth of your bag. It will also help to keep you warmer since clothing worn during the day may be damp from exertion.

Mid layers

Mid layers are for insulating. They work by trapping your body heat to keep you warm. The type of mid layer to use will vary based on the conditions. Fleece and wool are good options for breathability and their ability to insulate even when wet. Down or synthetic insulated jackets are the most popular choice for mid layers. Down has the best warmth to weight ratio, and it compresses smaller than synthetic insulation for packability.

For rainy conditions, synthetic might be a better choice since it insulates better than down when wet. Mid layers with full zippers are handy for being able to get them on and off easily.

Outer layers

Outer layers are for rain, wind and snow protection. A waterproof rain jacket is a must for backpacking in the Pacific Northwest. Even if it's not raining, a rain jacket can help to block wind and retain body warmth. Add rain pants or a rain skirt (yes, they exist!) when the forecast calls for wet or cold weather. Breathability is important in rain gear, otherwise, you can get saturated by sweating inside it. The most breathable options tend to be expensive but are often more durable. Look for items with vents such as pit zips, and sealed seams to keep rain out.

Additional options for outer layers include wind shells and soft shells. Wind shells are lightweight and water-resistant, best for blocking wind and light rain. Soft shells are highly breathable and good at blocking wind, but they are bulkier to pack and aren't waterproof.

HATS, GLOVES, GAITERS

Even on summer trips, a lightweight hat and pair of gloves are essential in case the temperature takes a plunge. In colder conditions, consider wool or fleece-lined hats, insulated gloves and a scarf or neck gaiter for extra warmth.

Tip: place damp clothing items in your sleeping bag at night and the warmth of your body will help them to dry.

Footwear

Thankfully, heavy and clunky leather boots are no longer the only choice for backpacking footwear. What you choose should be based upon the type of backpacking you do and what you find to be most comfortable. All feet are different, and what works for others may not be the best for you.

TYPES OF FOOTWEAR

Hiking boots are the most durable option and provide the most protection for your feet, with ankle support, stiffer soles and overall sturdy construction. They are generally recommended when you'll be carrying moderate to heavy loads and/or traversing rough terrain. They tend to be heavier and less breathable, and usually need to be broken in before a trip.

Hiking shoes are the middle ground between hiking boots and trail runners. While some styles are simply low-cut versions of sturdy hiking boots, most models are lighter and more flexible than boots. They tend to be slightly stiffer (and heavier) than trail running shoes. Hiking shoes are available in both waterproof and non-waterproof styles.

Trail running shoes are becoming increasingly popular, especially with thru-hikers on long distance trails due to their high level of comfort and lighter weight. Most models are non-waterproof, utilizing mesh in the upper for breathability and faster drying time. Due to the lighter materials used, they tend to not last as long as boots or shoes.

IMPORTANT FEATURES

Fit: Well-fitting footwear is critical to comfort on the trail. Take the time to get fitted and try on several pairs to find the best fit for you. Plan to try on shoes later in the day after your feet swell, and use the socks you'll wear while hiking. If you use aftermarket insoles, be sure to bring them when getting fitted. Walk around to get a good feel for fit, and if a store has an incline or simulated rock to use, try it out to make sure your toes don't hit the end of the shoe on a decline. How you lace your shoes can have an impact on fit as well. Look up lacing tips for accommodating various fit issues.

Waterproof versus non-waterproof: Consider wearing waterproof shoes or boots in cooler wet weather to keep your feet warm and dry. Otherwise, there can be significant advantages to wearing non-waterproof footwear for three-season use. They tend to have mesh uppers, which increases breathability to keep your feet cooler and are much less likely to cause blisters due to sweaty feet. They also dry faster than waterproof shoes.

Traction is extremely important to keep from slipping on the trail. Look for footwear with good tread (large lugs spaced across the bottom) and a "sticky" rubber outsole.

Weight: the saying "one pound on your feet equals five pounds on your back" is true. Carrying more weight on your feet uses more energy and can lead to muscle fatigue, so look for the lightest option in whichever type of footwear you choose.

SOCKS

A great sock may save your feet from blisters when paired with a comfortable shoe or boot.

Fabric: Most hiking socks use merino wool mixed with spandex for stretch and fit. Wool wicks moisture well (preventing sweaty feet), doesn't retain smells as much as synthetics, and provides good cushioning. Synthetic polyester or nylon socks are another good option. They tend to be more durable and faster drying, but do have a tendency to hold onto odor longer. Avoid cotton, which doesn't wick moisture and stays wet longer.

Sizing: Make sure to get the right size – socks that are too small will tend to slip down and may lead to pressure points, while socks that are too large can bunch up and cause blisters. Cushioning adds comfort but it also adds warmth. In cooler weather, the warmth may be needed, but it can lead to sweating in hot weather.

Height: Choose the height for a sock based on the conditions and footwear they will be worn with. To prevent skin from rubbing on footwear, keep the height of the sock above all parts of the shoe. Crew socks are the most popular option, providing coverage of your ankle and the lower portion of your calf. While good for wearing with hiking boots in most seasons, they can be a bit warm on a hot day. Ankle socks work well with hiking shoes, trail runners and some low-cut boots.

Toiletries

While personal hygiene when backpacking doesn't meet the same level of cleanliness as when you are at home, it is possible to feel relatively clean while taking minimal supplies.

> Tip: Animals are attracted to scented toiletry products, so choose unscented whenever possible. Otherwise, plan to store these items away from camp at night.

Dental hygiene: For keeping your teeth clean, a toothbrush may be all you need. Add a travel-size tube of toothpaste if you prefer to use it, and cut off a small amount of floss to bring along for the ultimate in mouth cleanliness.

Hair: Depending on the type of hair you have, a comb, brush or hair ties can help to keep wild tresses under control. For longer trips, or if your hair tends to get oily, no-rinse shampoo and dry shampoo are good options for cleaning your hair without harming the environment with soapy residues.

Body: At the end of each day, taking a quick sponge bath with a pack towel or wipes can get rid of most of the sweat and grime accumulated while hiking. Being outdoors all day and overnight can dry out your skin, so consider bringing body lotion.

Sun protection: Protect your skin (and lips) from damaging sun rays with sunscreen and lip balm.

Chafing ointment: Friction caused by movement can create chafing in areas where skin rubs together, and ointments or glide-type products can mitigate this troublesome issue.

Nail clippers: for keeping your fingernails and toenails snag-free.

Menstruation supplies: bring tampons or pads and a plastic bag for carrying out after use. Menstruation cups are also a good option for use in the backcountry since the waste from them can be buried in a cathole. And no, bears are not attracted to the scent... that's an old myth.

BATHROOM KIT

Build a simple kit with a few supplies and using the bathroom in the backcountry will be a breeze!

Trowel: a small trowel is essential for digging catholes for pooping. Trowels with serrated edges are useful for cutting through roots and solid ground. Ultralight trowels that weigh less than an ounce are a popular option for backpacking.

Toilet paper or wipes: bringing a little more than you need is better than not bringing enough.

Pack out kit: add a sealable plastic bag (odor-proof is a good option) for packing out toilet paper, wipes, and used menstration products. To hide the contents, use a pet waste bag and place that inside the sealable bag. Another option is to cover the outside of the bag with duct tape.

Bidet: A portable bidet that can be used for backpacking is basically a bottle with a spray head. Options include all-in-one sets with a bottle and spray head that nest together, or you can save some pack space and purchase a spray head designed to fit standard water bottles.

Pee cloth: While a bandana can be used effectively as a pee cloth, there are specialty products designed to be antimicrobial, with waterproof outers and snaps for carrying the pee cloth on your pack. Both are fantastic alternatives to using toilet paper for peeing, saving you the trouble of packing out more waste.

Hand sanitizer: One form of personal hygiene to not skip out on while backpacking is keeping your hands clean after doing your business in the backcountry. Keep a small bottle of sanitizer in your bathroom kit to remind you to use it.

> Learn how to lessen the impact of personal hygiene practices in the **Backcountry Bathroom** and **Personal Hygiene** section on pages 58-59.

Electronics

While backpacking is great for getting away from being "plugged in," there are a few electronics that can be useful on trips.

SMARTPHONES

Most backcountry sites will not have cell service, but a smartphone is still a useful tool for backpacking. One of the best uses is for navigation. There are many apps that will allow you to upload routes for a trip and track your hike, such as Gaia GPS. These apps can show you where you are on the trail, an invaluable tool while hiking. Just be sure to also carry paper maps and don't rely solely on your phone for navigation purposes since electronics can unexpectedly fail at the worst times. Additional apps can be useful for identifying features including wildflowers and nearby peaks, as well as for learning how to tie knots or adminster first aid. Reading e-books and storing trip info that can be accessed offline are additional ways to use your phone while backpacking.

SOS / PERSONAL LOCATOR DEVICES

These satellite devices can provide peace of mind for staying connected via texting, but also can alert search and rescue responders in case of an emergency. Look for models with two-way communication capabilities so you can provide important info to responders. Some devices even allow for pulling current weather forecasts based on your location. Annual or monthly service plans are usually required.

BATTERY BACKUP DEVICES

Useful for recharging everything from a smartphone, to an SOS device, a headlamp, and even a camera, look for a portable battery backup device that has enough power to work for your needs. And don't forget to take the cords for connecting to each device. Solar panels aren't as reliable as electric devices since they need hours of direct sun to recharge.

CAMERAS

If you are looking for an upgrade to using a phone for photos, small and lightweight mirrorless cameras are a great option for gaining more control over your photography. For carrying the camera while hiking, options include holsters that strap onto a pack's hip belt, or clips for attaching a camera to a backpack strap. To avoid dust and damage from rain, look for a camera that is weather-sealed and consider carrying a rain cover that fits over your camera. Add an ultralight tabletop-style tripod for group selfies, night sky photography, and long exposure shots.

> Battery saving tips: keep your phone on airplane mode while hiking and backpacking so it isn't constantly pinging for service (and running your battery down), and place electronics in your sleeping bag on cold nights.

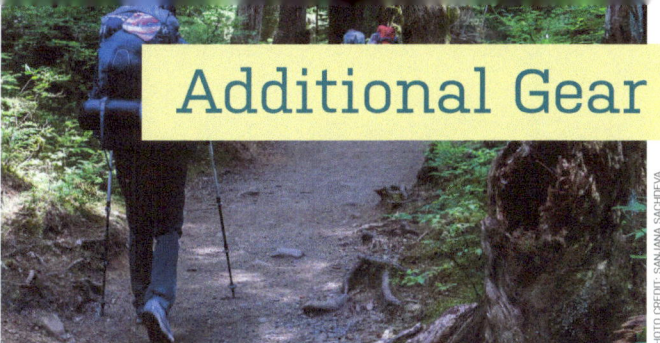

Additional Gear

TREKKING POLES

Trekking poles are notably useful for backpacking, providing stability on the trail and reducing the impact of carrying a loaded backpack. They utilize upper body strength to push up steep ascents, and provide stability and control on descents, helping to reduce the impact on your lower body (especially knees) and prevent falls. And on uneven terrain, during stream crossings, or on muddy trails, they provide added points of contact to improve traction and balance.

WHAT TO LOOK FOR IN A TREKKING POLE

Pole structure: There are three types of poles: collapsible, fixed length or foldable. Collapsible poles have multiple sections that telescope and use locking mechanisms for setting a variable height. These are the most durable type due to the overlapping pole shafts which add strength to the structure. Fixed length poles (i.e. ski poles) are typically not used for backpacking since they aren't as packable or adustable. Folding-style poles pack down the smallest and are often the lightest option.

Material: aluminum and carbon fiber are the most common materials for trekking pole shafts, and both are good options depending on what your needs are. Carbon fiber is the lightest (and most expensive) option, but they are more likely to break under high pressure. Aluminum is slightly heavier, but less expensive and more durable over time.

Locking mechanisms: For adjustable poles, look for easy to use lever-style locking mechanisms.

Handles: Materials used for handles include foam, cork, and rubber. Cork is comfortable to hold, doesn't absorb moisture from sweat, and conforms to the shape of your hands better than other materials. Foam absorbs moisture and has a soft feel but isn't as durable long term. Rubber reduces vibration and insulates against cold, but in warm weather, moisture can make them slippery and cause friction. Whichever material you choose, it should feel comfortable in your hands.

USING TREKKING POLES

Place hands through the straps from the bottom and grasp the handle. This helps prevent gripping the pole too tightly. When holding the poles, your elbows should be at a 90 degree angle. On steep uphill sections, shorten the poles slightly, and on descents, lengthen them. For optimum pole strength, keep both sections of collapsible poles at the same length.

BACKPACKING CHAIRS

A camp chair is a luxury item that may not be necessary for some people. However, if you have back, hip or other issues when you sit on the ground for prolonged periods, a backpacking chair can be a comfort item worth carrying.

Collapsible chairs are the most comfortable option for sitting off the ground and being able to fully rest your back. To set up, simply unfold the poles and snap them together, then add the fabric cover. An added bonus of this style of chair is that it can hold gear while unpacking your backpack, or for carrying your food and stove to the backcountry kitchen. They are also good for storing gear off the ground in a tent vestibule.

Air mattress kits are fabric sleeves that fit around an air pad folded into a chair shape, providing back support while sitting low to the ground. Make sure the kit works with your air pad when purchasing.

Stadium-style chairs are made of fabric with added foam for comfort and fold in half for carrying. While they provide a way to sit on the ground with back support and don't require set up other than tightening straps on the sides, they tend to be heavier than other options and are bulky to pack.

Sit seats are the lightest and smallest option. While they don't offer back support, they provide cushioning when sitting on rocks and logs. They can also be used outside a tent door to protect your knees when getting in and out of your tent.

Navigation

Insulation

Sun Protection

Illumination

Fire Starter

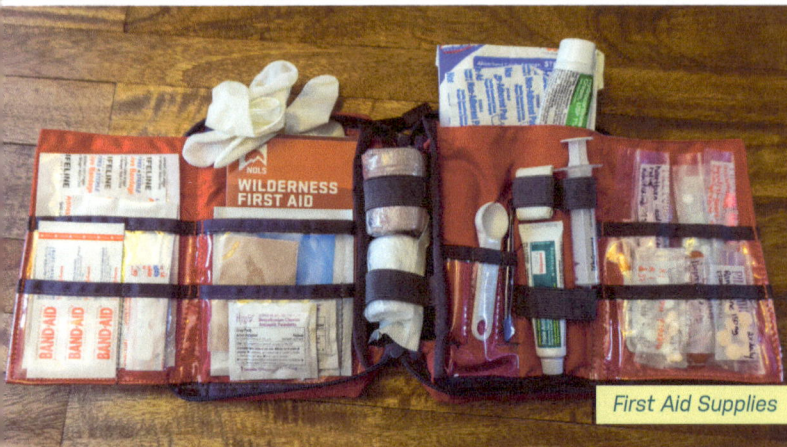

First Aid Supplies

Extra Water

Repair Kit

Extra Food

Emergency Shelter

The Ten Essentials

The premise behind taking essentials on hiking and backpacking trips is to be prepared for accidents and emergencies. While you may not need all of these items on every trip, they can make a big difference when they are needed. On backpacking trips, make sure to stash these essentials in your daypack for hikes away from camp.

NAVIGATION: Always carry a paper map! Maps are especially useful when you aren't sure which trail to take at a junction or to know what type of terrain to expect. Even if you are familiar with the trail, a map will be important if you need to get off trail for any reason. Learn how to read the map and orient yourself to the landscape.

SUN PROTECTION: It can be easy to overlook the need for sun protection with so many grey, cloudy days in the Pacific Northwest. But clouds are much better at blocking visible light than damaging UV rays. At higher altitudes, sun protection is particularly important. The air is thinner and cleaner, which leads to higher UV exposure. Additionally, UV light bounces off surfaces such as sand, snow, and water. There are many hikers who have learned the hard way that they should have put sunscreen IN their nostrils after a day on snowpack! For the best protection, use sunglasses, hats, sunscreen with SPF 15 or higher that protects against both UVB and UBA rays, and lip balm with SPF. For areas with significant sun exposure, consider wearing long sleeve shirts and pants with UV protection.

INSULATION: Even on the sunniest of days, the weather can change abruptly in the backcountry, so bringing extra layers to deal with varying conditions is always a good idea. In the Pacific Northwest, a rain jacket should go on every trip, as well as a lightweight insulated jacket or puffy, a hat, and a light pair of gloves.

ILLUMINATION: Light is important in order to move around safely at night. It may also provide psychological comfort should you find yourself in a stressful and dark situation. Several companies make very good LED headlamps and flashlights that are affordable, water resistant, bright, and efficient. Like all gear, know how to use it before hitting the trail, and check the battery level and/or bring extra batteries.

FIRST-AID SUPPLIES: The size of your first aid kit will depend upon the length of your journey and the size of the group that it is meant to treat. Ideally, each backpacker will carry their own first aid kit with items specific to their needs. *See the Basic First Aid section on page 50 for more info.*

FIRE STARTER: The ability to start a fire can be a literal lifesaver in an emergency situation. But it's not always the easiest task in the soggier areas of the Pacific Northwest. Essential gear for starting a fire includes a lighter or waterproof matches and dry tinder of some type. For economical and lightweight tinder options, bring lint from a clothes dryer; coat cotton balls in petroleum jelly; or add wood shavings to unscented candle wax.

REPAIR KIT & TOOLS: A multi-tool and/or pocketknife can be one of the most valuable items that you will bring with you. They can assist in cutting food, sawing wood, splitting a bandage, or fixing a zipper. Scissors are a particularly useful feature to have in a multi-tool. For a repair kit, duct tape works well for almost everything, at least temporarily. A needle and thread can help with repairing tears in shoes or boots, clothing, tents, and backpacks.

EXTRA FOOD: In addition to your planned snacks or meals, bring a small amount of extra food in case a hike or trip is unexpectedly extended. Items that don't need cooking are best, including trail bars, nuts, and dried fruit.

EXTRA WATER: Always bring plenty of water and a way to treat water from natural sources using filters, purifiers, or chemicals when you need more. In general, plan to drink a half liter of water for every hour of moderate exercise, increasing the amount in hot weather or during periods of intense exertion.

EMERGENCY SHELTER: The purpose of an emergency shelter is to assist with keeping a lost or injured person relatively warm and dry. When hiking away from camp while backpacking, it's a good idea to carry a lightweight emergency shelter in case you can't make it back to camp. Emergency blankets made of a thin reflective mylar material are commonly provided in survival kits for this purpose. Additional options include bivy sacks, tarps, and large plastic bags.

ONE MORE ESSENTIAL – COMMON SENSE: Keeping a level head and making well thought out decisions during emergency situations is your best ally in getting home safely. When feeling stressed, remember to breathe and use skills that you have practiced such as navigation, fire-starting, and first aid.

Skills

Trip Planning Basics

Trip planning can be intimidating, but it doesn't have to be. The process of researching a destination for backpacking can help you to feel more comfortable with exploring new places. Even with thorough trip planning, there's still plenty of discovery left for the actual backpacking experience. The goal is to be properly prepared and to avoid unexpected conditions or situations. The ten step planning process outlined here will help you to plan a trip based on your capabilities and interests.

STEP 1: DETERMINE TRIP LOCATION

Before choosing a destination for a backpacking trip, start with the basics. What time of year are you planning to go backpacking? There are many options in the Pacific Northwest for backpacking year round… or at least most of the year.

TIME OF YEAR

In the spring, low elevation locations are usually snow-free, but this time of year can also be quite rainy. It helps to have some flexibility in your schedule so you can take advantage of good weather when it happens. The high desert, which can be too hot for summer trips, is a good option in the spring since it gets sparce rainfall compared to the rest of the region.

Early summer will likely still have a fair amount of snow at higher elevations in the mountains, but mid-level elevations can be snow-free in May or June depending on the year's snowpack level.

Summer is prime backpacking time, usually mid-July through September. Most people prefer to backpack in the summer, as it's the only time of year to experience higher elevations without snow cover. Early summer is also when mosquitoes can be a problem (usually the first several weeks after snow melt), so know how to deal with them or where to go to avoid them.

As the weather starts to change in the fall, so do the colors of foliage, making this time of year great for trips to areas with brilliant fall color. There are fewer people on the trails this time of year as well.

Backpacking is also possible in the winter, although it can require special skills and gear to deal with snow and colder conditions.

RESOURCES FOR INFO ABOUT DESTINATIONS

How do you know where to go? Hiking and backpacking books are a good source for ideas, although you may find just as many possibilities searching online.

ONLINE RESOURCES

Since the places we backpack in are public lands managed by government agencies, their websites are a great resource for planning trips. *See the Land Managers & Ranger Stations sidebar on page 33.*

For Oregon and Washington, two online resources for hiking are the Washington Trails Association (wta.org) and Oregon Hikers (oregonhikers.org) websites. Both offer extensive information and trip descriptions, and although they are geared more to hiking than backpacking, they can still provide helpful info needed for planning a backpacking trip.

Additional websites that offer hiking and backpacking destination info are the Outdoor Project (outdoorproject.com), REI's Hiking Project (hikingproject.com), and Clever Hiker (cleverhiker.com).

SOCIAL MEDIA

Seeing trip reports from other people's trips can be a great motivator for finding out more about a destination on your own. There are many groups on Facebook dedicated to hiking, with the active groups getting updated with posts every day. It's also a good way to learn the current conditions for specific areas.

Backpacking on the Washington coast

PHOTO CREDIT: LORI BROWN

STEP 2: SET TRIP PARAMETERS

Before you determine the type of backpacking trip to plan, take the time to think about what you want out of the trip. Just as in the mantra "hike your own hike," you should "plan your own plan." While others may influence where you choose to go, you should plan the trip according to your needs. Attempting to stick to a plan that is unrealistic for you can be frustrating, or worse, lead to a trip that makes backpacking seem like a miserable chore. Instead, learn how to plan the type of trip that fits your backpacking style.

BACKPACKING STYLES

Recognizing how you like to backpack can help you plan the most enjoyable trip for you. Before starting out, take some time to consider your goals and interests.

Relaxing at camp on an early spring trip

For many backpackers, especially beginners, a balance of hiking and spending time in camp is an enjoyable way to backpack, as well as being less strenuous. Setting up a basecamp will allow you to hike fewer miles with a heavy pack, have a leisurely breakfast, and then head out on day hikes before returning to camp each night. If you are spending more time at camp, you might want to bring a backpacking chair, extra cookware, or reading material.

Others might prefer to do more hiking, covering as many miles as they can before stopping to camp for the night. In this case,

Hiking-focused trip in the North Cascades

bringing as little as possible is the goal, keeping pack weight to a minimum so that you can hike longer distances. This approach will allow you to see more of an area, and would be suitable for longer loop or shuttle trips.

For those interested in photographing scenery and wildlife, a trip plan might include shorter hikes to allow for carrying camera equipment and more frequent stops for photo opportunities. Photographers usually have a different type of schedule on backpacking trips. Capturing the best light of the day often means getting up before dawn, or being in the right location as the sun sets. And if you are into night photography, that could mean shooting at 2am in order to capture the star-studded sky.

Perhaps you have young children and are hoping to share the outdoors as a family. Your style, at least for the first several trips, may be to plan single night trips accessible via easier hikes, stopping often for breaks.

Regardless of which style you prefer, spending time in the wilderness is an amazing experience. The goal of this book is to make backpacking more accessible to those without experience. Over time, your style will likely evolve as you gain more profiency with your gear and the skills needed for backpacking.

LEVEL OF DIFFICULTY

Parameters that determine the difficulty of a trip include the number of nights spent, miles and elevation gain per day, and the type of terrain that you'll be hiking in.

Consider how much distance and elevation gain to cover on each day. In general, plan on a pace of around two miles an hour, adding an hour for every 1,000 feet of elevation gain. Hiking speed can vary considerably based on your individual fitness level, the weight of your pack, and the terrain. For example, does the trail have any steep and rocky ascents or difficult water crossings? Or is it a well-groomed trail with gradual elevation gain?

It's a good idea to start with an easier approach on trips until you are comfortable with your gear and the skills needed for backpacking. Even seasoned backpackers should consider beginning each backpacking season with an easy trip to test new gear and get familiar again with the processes of backpacking.

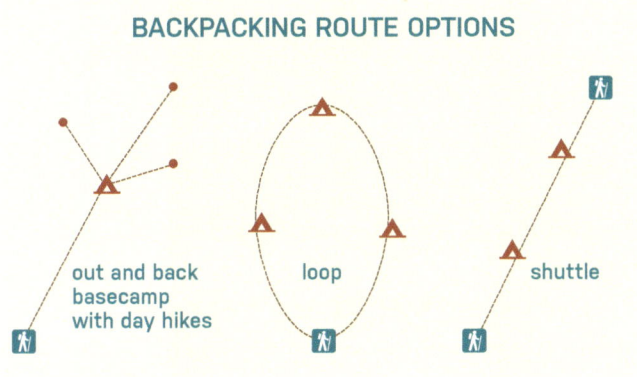

TYPE OF ROUTE

For planning a route and campsites, do you prefer to do an out-and-back, a shuttle, or a loop hike? Out-and-back trips are often the easiest since they offer the opportunity to set up a basecamp and day hike from there instead of hiking with a fully loaded pack each day. Loop hikes offer the ability to cover more miles, requiring moving campsites from night to night in order to complete the loop. Like loop trips, shuttle trips allow you to cover more miles but require more planning, with a need to shuttle cars to both trailheads.

GROUP SIZE

To determine the optimal group size, consider area regulations and campsite availability. Most wilderness areas limit group size for hiking and camping to 12 people. However, it would be very difficult to find campsites suitable for such a large group. Backcountry campsites vary greatly in size, with most being optimal for 1-4 people. It is possible to find sites suitable for groups of 6-8 backpackers, but it's not as common.

LAND MANAGERS & RANGER STATIONS

Obtaining backcountry permits at a ranger station

Backpacking destinations are located on public lands managed by agencies, including the U.S. Forest Service, National Park Service, and the Bureau of Land Management. These agencies provide information about the trails and backcountry campsites within their areas. Check their websites for info about regulations and permits as well as current conditions and alerts that may be in effect.

Most backcountry areas in Oregon and Washington are managed by the U.S. Forest Service (fs.fed.us), including national forests and designated wilderness areas. The National Park Service (nps.gov) manages the Olympic National Park, Mount Rainier National Park, North Cascades National Park, and Crater Lake National Park. Fewer backpacking opportunities exist in Bureau of Land Management areas (blm.gov).

Don't be shy about calling park rangers to answer questions you have. They may be more up-to-date on current conditions and able to provide info not found online. Ultimately, if you are well informed before you head out on a trip, you are less likely to need their assistance once out in the backcountry.

STEP 3: PERMITS, PASSES, AND REGULATIONS

When you are considering a backpacking destination, you'll need to know what type of passes and permits are required and what the regulations for an area are. Check online or contact ranger stations at land management agencies for your destination to learn more.

PERMITS

Permits are required for backcountry camping in many national forest, wilderness and national park locations. Each area has different regulations for backcountry camping, so it's important to understand what they are when you are planning a trip.

Filling out a self-issued wilderness permit

Self-issued permits are the most common type, with self-registration boxes located at trailheads or at wilderness boundaries on the trail. Some areas have become so popular and overused that advance permits are required. It's often possible to obtain these types of permits via walk-in registration the day of or before a trip, but others may require submitting an application. The most coveted areas may be permitted via a lottery system and can be quite difficult to obtain. Knowing which type of permit is required is a crucial part of the trip planning process.

Also determine where the permit should be displayed. Self-issued permits filled out at trailheads (common in national forests and wilderness areas) are for hikers as well as backpackers and should be carried with you at all times. Permits that require online or in person registration are often required to be displayed on the outside of your tent so it can be checked by rangers on patrol in the backcountry.

Backcountry permit displayed on a tent

PASSES

Passes may be required for entry and/or parking at trailheads, depending on the location. The Northwest Forest Pass is the most common type needed for backpacking locations in Oregon and Washington, although a National Park Pass may be required at national parks.

On state-managed land a state parks pass may be required – although very few state parks allow overnight backcountry camping.

While some areas have pay stations for passes, many do not so it's good to know before you go. Many of the required passes can be purchased online, at retailers, or at ranger stations.

REGULATIONS

Wilderness areas have regulations that vary by location. The regulations cover rules about group size, campfires, food storage, campsite locations, length of stay and more. Be familiar with what the regulations are for the area you plan to go to and be prepared to follow them.

STEP 4: PREPARE AND PRINT MAPS

Maps are critical to have once you are on the trail, but they are also an essential part of trip planning. By thoroughly reviewing a map before your trip, you'll become familiar with the trails you plan to hike, identify potential campsite locations, water access, potential hazards, and more.

Start by locating the trailhead you plan to begin your trip at, then review the trails you'll travel. Also familiarize yourself with

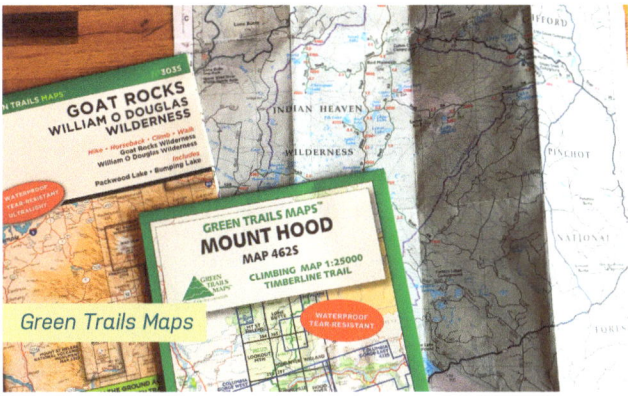

Green Trails Maps

the trails that cross your intended route in case you need to find an alternate way to exit the trail in an emergency.

Large multi-fold maps for national forests, wilderness areas and national parks can be purchased at outdoor retailers, ranger stations, or online. These maps provide a big overview of an area, which is great for getting familiar with a new destination, but they usually cover more area than you need on the trail and the scale may not provide enough details for your trip.

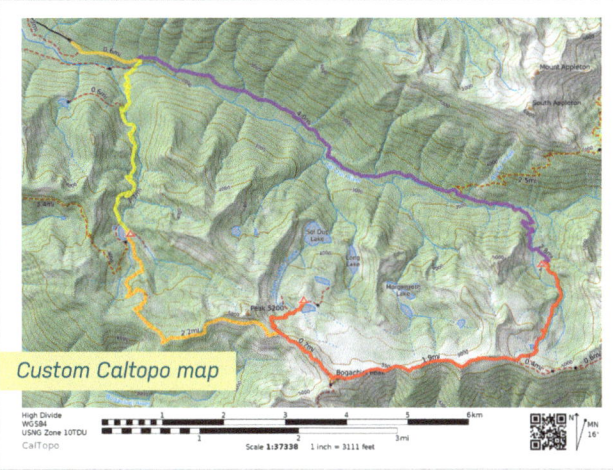

Custom Caltopo map

Smaller format paper maps that are more suitable for backpacking include USGS maps and Green Trails maps. Available for purchase at some outdoor retailers or online, these maps provide more detail than large scale maps and are easier to use on trail due to their portable format. Green Trails maps contain current trail and access info, point-to-point mileage, and points of interest, as well as local contact information. Some also provide established campsite locations. Green Trails also offers ultralight folding maps for popular destination areas that are waterproof and tear-resistant. USGS maps are printed on larger paper and don't provide as many details but are available for all areas within U.S. Forest Services boundaries.

Online mapping tools such as Caltopo (caltopo.com) and Gaia (gaiagps.com) offer the ability to create custom maps. Add line segments to highlight your route, and waypoints for trailheads, campsite locations, destinations, or other features. After adding trail segments, you'll be able to view data for mileage, elevation gain, terrain, exposure, and more. Keep in mind that the data from online tools may not be as accurate as guidebooks. After creating your map, you'll be able to share it with others and save files for printing. Gaia also has a smartphone app for use on trail.

For more info on Navigation, see page 47.

STEP 6: PLANNING FOR GROUPS

When planning a group trip, consider the experience level of the participants. Trips for beginners may need to be based on an easier style than a trip planned for experienced backpackers. Find out whether the group prefers to hike long days covering many miles, or whether they prefer to spend more time at camp relaxing... or a mix of both. Ask about previous backpacking experience, first aid training, or other expertise. And discuss the type of gear needed for a trip and whether or not anyone prefers to share gear with others to help lighten their loads.

Clear communication is key for success on group trips. When everyone has an understanding of what a trip will encompass, misunderstandings are less likely to happen. Share the trip itinerary with everyone and hold pre-trip meetings to go over logistics and discuss trip expectations. Group trip plans should also include carpooling logistics and a list of any necessary fees.

STEP 5: DOCUMENT THE TRIP PLAN

Documenting a trip plan may seem like an unnecessary step, but there are several benefits to doing so. You'll get a better sense of the level of difficulty required for the trip you are planning, have a clear way to communicate the plan to other trip members, and you'll have a detailed trip itinerary to leave with someone in case of an emergency.

To begin documenting a trip plan, create a daily itinerary that includes trailheads, hiking trails, campsite locations, and the mileage and elevation gain for each day.

Additional data to document can include information about permits, passes and regulations, and links to maps, weather reports, and land manager websites.

TRAVEL PLANS

For longer distance trips, include travel logistics in your documentation. For example, longer drives to trailheads may emcompass planned stops for meals, stopping at a ranger station for permits, or spending the night at a hotel or campground before beginning a trip.

Food for a four day trip

STEP 7: PREP GEAR & FOOD

Before you head out on a trip, take the time to check your gear. Fix anything that needs repairs and replenish consumable items such as spare batteries, toilet paper or wipes, toothpaste, and fuel for your backpacking stove.

Create a packing list that includes everything needed on a backpacking trip. While there are many lists online that can be utilized, creating a custom list based on your gear will help make sure that you don't forget anything. Once you have a complete list, do a practice load with your backpack and try it on... sometimes you may need to re-pack to get the load balanced properly.

trip plan template

potential dates
#days/nights
group size
type of trip
high point
passes
permits
notes
maps
weather

Itinerary	miles	elev. gain	elev. loss
day 1			
day 2			
day 3			
day 4			
distance + elevation totals			

Location & Emergency Contact Info

trailhead
location
USFS info
ranger station
closest towns
emergency contact

Driving Directions

from/to	directions	drive time	distance	carpool

Sample trip form template

For meal planning, start by creating a list of the number of meals needed. It's easy to over or under estimate the amount of food needed, so it can be helpful to lay out all of your food in rows for each day of a trip. This way, you can visually see how much you have.

To save space, replace bulky packaging with lightweight plastic bags. Also consider the food storage method you'll need to use and plan to bring the appropriate gear for it.

STEP 8: WEATHER FORECASTS & CURRENT CONDITIONS

It's important to know what your preferences are regarding weather conditions. Some people don't mind rain on a trip, while others prefer to go when it's much less likely. The same goes for hot weather, or colder conditions. Knowing the expected daytime high temperatures, overnight lows, and chance of rain or snow can make a trip more enjoyable for all.

Rapidly changing conditions in the North Cascades

For weather forecasts, one of the most reliable sources is the National Weather Service website (weather.gov). For the most accurate forecast for your destination, click on the desired area directly on the map, or by entering latitudinal and longitudinal coordinates. This method is better than checking a forecast for nearby cities since it will take in account the elevation and specific conditions of the location. Forecasts are continually updated, with the most accurate info available a few days in advance, so keep checking to see if conditions have changed before leaving on a trip.

Thick layer of wildfire smoke in the Wallowas

For higher elevations, another resource for weather is Mountain Forecast (mountain-forecast.org). Select the range, then a specific peak, and finally, the elevation you'll be at to see expected conditions for your location.

CURRENT CONDITIONS

Throughout the year, many trails experience changes due to storms or other conditions. To find out the current conditions for a specific area, contact a ranger station for information about trail or road closures, wildfires, or other conditions that may impact your trip.

WILDFIRES

Wildfires are a common occurrence during the Pacific Northwest's dry summers, and some years, they can impact vast areas not just with fire, but also with widespread smoke. New fires can start unexpectedly, especially during thunderstorms. Know what the current fire dangers are by checking with ranger stations. In addition, there are many online resources for tracking current wildfires and air quality.

INSECTS

Biting insects such as mosquitoes and black flies may impact when you choose to schedule a backpacking trip. Generally, the annual hatch happens within the first few weeks after the snow melts in higher elevations. In Oregon and Washington, this tends to be anytime from June to August depending on the elevation and location. Early to mid-July is typically when most hatches occur in the mountains.

Wearing a head net while doing camp chores

COASTAL TIDES

If you are backpacking along the coast, tides should be taken into consideration since some areas are accessible only at low tide. Check online sources (such as tidesandcurrents.noaa.gov), or pick up a printed tide table at locations along the coast, including state parks and ranger stations.

Low tide at the Point of Arches

BACKUP PLANS

Have a backup plan in case you need to cancel or reschedule a trip due to weather or other conditions. The Pacific Northwest has many types of climates and it is often possible to choose another location with better conditions if your original location doesn't work out. For example, in the spring, the high desert is often rain-free while western locations are drenched. Or, later in the season, wildfires may impact one part of the region but not another. Having multiple locations to choose from can make the difference from being able to go on a trip versus cancelling.

STEP 9: SAFETY & EMERGENCY PLANNING

Prior to departing on your trip, be sure to leave your itinerary with a trusted person. This individual should be given the date that you plan to leave, the date that you plan to arrive back to the trailhead, and the date and time that they should call emergency officials if you have not returned. Itineraries should include the names and contact info for all trip members.

You should also include details of where you will be hiking and where you plan on camping, and leave a copy of a marked map when possible. Additional details including the make and model of the vehicles that will be left at the trailhead can come in handy should search and rescue become necessary.

Finally, remember to contact your trusted person when you return from your trip. Having a search team go out after you because you forgot to make a phone call is an expensive and embarrassing error.

To be prepared for emergencies, have each person on a trip fill out an emergency contact form. Optional medical info that is provided could be critical in case first aid or rescue is required.

Also consider taking a personal locator beacon, such as the Garmin InReach or Spot. These types of devices have SOS buttons that can be pressed in case of an emergency and will send a message to the authorities with your location. Some allow two-way texting so you can communicate with emergency responders, or for staying in touch with loved ones.

STEP 10: FINAL LOGISTICS

Forecasts can change overnight, so check the weather again before you head out. If wildfires or other conditions exist, check those as well.

Don't forget to take printed driving directions. Cell service is usually not available on the way to the trailhead, and directions from apps are not always reliable, especially on Forest Roads.

Now it's time to get out into the backcountry, stay safe, and most of all, have fun!

Trip Itinerary

If you have not heard from me by (time) _____ on (day) _____ of (month) _____, call search and rescue at 911 and report me as overdue. Be prepared to provide search and rescue with ALL of the information in this trip plan.

Trip name

Trailhead

County, State, Sheriff #

Nearest town

Ranger station

Date & time of departure

Estimated date & time of return

day   trail, route, campsite area

participant   age   mobile phone number

vehicle make / model   color   license plate

Sample trip itinerary and emergency/personal information forms

EMERGENCY/PERSONAL INFORMATION

Today's Date: _____

First and Last Name: _____ Middle Initial: _____
Address:_____
City: _____ State: _____ Zip:_____
Phone Numbers: Cell: _____ Home: _____
Email address: _____

Primary Emergency Contact
Individual to be contacted in an emergency or other urgent situation
Name: _____ Relationship:_____
Phone: _____ Secondary Phone: _____

Secondary Emergency Contact
Individual to be contacted if primary emergency contact is unavailable:
Name: _____ Relationship:_____
Phone: _____ Secondary Phone:_____

Other information
Birthdate: _____
Medical Conditions: _____
_____
_____
Allergies: _____
_____
Medications: _____
_____
Other: _____
_____

Information provided on this page is for reference and emergency use only. Its purpose is to facilitate/expedite administrative and EMS functions. All data on this form is protected by The Privacy Act of 1974.

Leave No Trace Seven Principles

Plan Ahead and Prepare

+ Know the regulations and special concerns for the area you'll visit.
+ Prepare for extreme weather, hazards, and emergencies.
+ Schedule your trip to avoid times of high use.
+ Visit in small groups when possible. Consider splitting larger groups into smaller groups.
+ Repackage food to minimize waste.
+ Use a map and compass to eliminate the use of marking paint, rock cairns or flagging.

Travel and Camp on Durable Surfaces

+ Durable surfaces include established trails and campsites, rock, gravel, dry grasses or snow.
+ Protect riparian areas by camping at least 200 feet from lakes and streams.
+ Good campsites are found, not made. Altering a site is not necessary.

In popular areas:

+ Concentrate use on existing trails and campsites.
+ Walk single file in the middle of the trail, even when wet or muddy.
+ Keep campsites small. Focus activity in areas where vegetation is absent.

In pristine areas:

+ Disperse use to prevent the creation of campsites and trails.
+ Avoid places where impacts are just beginning.

Dispose of Waste Properly

+ Pack it in, pack it out. Inspect your campsite and rest areas for trash or spilled foods. Pack out all trash, leftover food and litter.
+ Deposit solid human waste in catholes 6 to 8 inches deep, at least 200 feet from water, camp and trails. Cover and disguise the cathole when finished.
+ Pack out toilet paper and hygiene products.
+ To wash yourself or your dishes, carry water 200 feet away from streams or lakes and use small amounts of biodegradable soap. Scatter strained dishwater.

Text on pages 40-41 © 1999 by the Leave No Trace Center for Outdoor Ethics: www.LNT.org.

Minimize Campfire Impacts

+ Campfires can cause lasting impacts to the backcountry. Use a lightweight stove for cooking and enjoy a candle lantern for light.
+ Where fires are permitted, use established fire rings, fire pans, or mound fires.
+ Keep fires small. Only use sticks from the ground that can be broken by hand.
+ Burn all wood and coals to ash, put out campfires completely, then scatter cool ashes.

Leave What You Find

+ Preserve the past: examine, but do not touch cultural or historic structures and artifacts.
+ Leave rocks, plants and other natural objects as you find them.
+ Avoid introducing or transporting non-native species.
+ Do not build structures, furniture, or dig trenches.

Respect Wildlife

+ Observe wildlife from a distance. Do not follow or approach them.
+ Never feed animals. Feeding wildlife damages their health, alters natural behaviors, and exposes them to predators and other dangers.
+ Protect wildlife and your food by storing rations and trash securely.
+ Control pets at all times, or leave them at home.
+ Avoid wildlife during sensitive times: mating, nesting, raising young, or winter.

Be Considerate of Other Visitors

+ Respect other visitors and protect the quality of their experience.
+ Be courteous. Yield to other users on the trail.
+ Step to the downhill side of the trail when encountering pack stock.
+ Take breaks and camp away from trails and other visitors.
+ Let nature's sounds prevail. Avoid loud voices and noises.

Physical Preparation

GETTING STARTED

The physical exertion of backpacking can be an intimidating factor when someone considers hitting the trail for the first time. Always consider your current fitness level and consult with your physician before undertaking a new workout.

Everyone starts out at a different skill level and that is why many of the trips described in this book have route options that will allow the ability to add on or take away mileage.

CONDITIONING

One of the best ways to get in condition for backpacking is to hike on a regular basis with a loaded pack. Start light and slowly add weight to your pack over time. A good beginning would be 10 pounds, increasing to 20-30 pounds, depending on what you expect your final pack weight to be. To build endurance, increase the distance and elevation gain done on day hikes and consider hiking multiple days in a row to prepare for longer trips. Since carrying a fully loaded pack will test your balance skills, hike in varied terrain, such as on rocky or muddy trails, and practice stream crossing skills.

Strength training exercises such as lunges, squats, and planks can work to build key muscle groups, which will not only make the hiking experience more pleasant, but it will reduce the risk of injury.

Building an aerobic base through activities like biking, running, or dancing to your favorite music in your living room can also help prepare for the physical endurance needed for backpacking.

STRETCHING

You may experience some muscular soreness as you begin physical conditioning for your upcoming trip. When people experience pain with backpacking it tends to affect the legs, hips, or back. Static stretching can help to release tension in the body and relieve pain in some of these key areas.

TRY THESE STRETCHES TO HELP WITH FLEXIBILITY AND PAIN. THEY ARE EASY TO DO BOTH AT HOME OR ON THE TRAIL.

To help loosen hamstrings, sit on the floor with the leg to be stretched out straight. Your other leg should be bent. Lean forward at the hips. You are doing it correctly if you feel a stretch under the thigh. Hold the stretch for 30 seconds. Repeat the stretch throughout the day.

Tightness of the hip flexors may also cause issues. To stretch this muscle begin in a half-kneeling position with one leg behind you. If you have trekking poles or a stick, you may hold them in front of you. Actively push the trekking poles or stick down into the ground. While keeping your body upright rotate your pelvis. Keeping your pelvis rotated and body upright, lean forward at the hips. Hold this position for no more than 2 seconds. Repeat.

To release tension in the calves stand facing a tree with your arms straight in front of you. Place your hands flat against a tree. Keep one leg forward, foot flat on the ground, and extend the other leg straight back. Try to lower your heel flat to the ground. Do not bend your back knee. Lean into the tree until you feel the stretch in the calf of the straight leg. Hold for 30 seconds and switch sides. Repeat throughout the day.

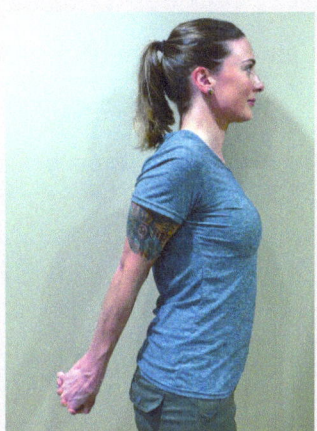

Sore shoulders are also a common complaint while backpacking. Keep in mind that a majority of your pack's weight should be supported by your hips. However, bearing some weight on the shoulders is inevitable. To stretch the shoulders and chest, lock your hands behind your back. With straight arms, raise your hands towards the sky until you feel a stretch. Do not raise any farther than what is a comfortable stretch.

Hiking Safety

REVIEW THE HIKE PLAN

Before starting the hike in, take a few minutes to go over the trip plan and review the trail map. Everyone in a group should be aware of the intended route, including the name of the trailhead, the trails to be hiked, location of trail junctions, and the preferred destination for setting up camp. This will help to ensure that no one gets lost, but if they do, they'll have an idea of where they've been and where they should be.

Some groups prefer to stick together at all times on hikes, but if some people prefer to hike at a slower or faster pace than others, make a plan for when you'll regroup. One option is to agree to wait at every trail junction, which also helps to prevent someone from taking the wrong trail at a junction. If there aren't any trail junctions on the route, agree to stop after a certain distance or time. It's a good idea to hike in groups of two or more, and always let someone know if you need to stop for any reason to avoid getting left behind.

Checking the map while looking for a campsite

KNOW WHERE YOU ARE

The best way to prevent getting lost is to always know where you are. Unless you know the area well, refer to your map often during the hike and make a mental note of all trail intersections as you pass them. Ideally, everyone on the trip will carry a map with them and be familiar with it. If you are using a GPS device or smartphone app, you can have it track you while you hike, and mark waypoints for locations along the trail that you want to remember.

Keeping an eye on changing weather while hiking

WEATHER

Rain: In many parts of the Pacific Northwest, one of your bigger weather worries may be rain. The region has earned a reputation for producing rain that can last for weeks. Be prepared with proper rain gear in the case of moisture. One of the more miserable mistakes that you can make is allowing your gear to get wet. Once soaked, it could be quite some time before you have the opportunity to dry out. If it begins to rain, your best option is to stop what you are doing and ensure that all gear will stay dry. Pack covers can work well in light rain showers but in a heavy rainstorm may not be enough to keep everything dry. Try waterproof stuff sacks, re-sealable plastic bags, or a trash bag lining the inside of your backpack. Once your pack is water-tight, open it only when necessary.

Lightning: In thunderstorms with lightning, know when to take action. You are within strike range when thunder and lightning are 30 seconds apart. Care for yourself by getting away from any tall, solitary trees. If you are in an exposed area, descend from ridge lines and get below tree line. Move away from water. Make yourself less prone to being struck by becoming the lowest object in your area. Crouching will allow you to be as small as possible while minimizing your body's contact with the ground. If you are hiking with a group, each member should spread out at least 25 feet. Remain in a safe area until 30 minutes after the last sound of thunder.

Cold weather: Hypothermia can be a risk in cool, wet weather and the best way to care for yourself is prevention. Be aware of your core temperature and take steps to stay warm. Simply moving will keep you warm in most situations. Hydration helps to regulate temperature, and it is important to continue drinking even in the cold. Heat water for a hot drink to warm up quickly.

Always know the signs of hypothermia, which are discussed in more depth under **Basic First Aid** on pages 50-51.

Hot weather: Avoid heat exhaustion, heat stroke, sunburn and dehydration on hot days by staying well hydrated, applying sunscreen often, and seeking shelter from the sun when needed. In extreme heat, avoid hiking during the hottest part of the day and in fully exposed areas. To cool off, dip a bandana in a stream or lake and place at the back of your neck. Consider hiking with a reflective umbrella on trails with full sun exposure during periods of hot weather.

Day hiking with essentials on a backpacking trip

Crossing a stream on logs

ALWAYS TAKE THE ESSENTIALS

On a backpacking trip where you'll be leaving camp to do day hikes, make sure to take essential items with you. Items to always carry include: navigation tools, water, food, first aid, additional layers, a headlamp, and an emergency shelter such as a tarp or bivy. If something happens and you are unable to make it back to your campsite, you should still be able to stay safe. Some backpacks have a detachable lid meant to be used as a day pack, or you can use your backpack and make it smaller by tightening the compression straps. Bringing an ultralight day pack on your trip for day hikes is another option. Some only weigh a few ounces and stuff into a built-in pouch.

STREAM CROSSINGS

Crossing small streams while hiking is fairly common, and it's usually easy to do without getting your feet wet. A few precautions will help to keep you dry and lessen the chances of slipping in. When crossing on rocks, test the stability of a rock before placing all of your weight on it. Once there, keep your weight centered over your standing leg while reaching out for the next step. Look for dry rocks sticking out of the water when possible, and watch out for slick algae-covered rocks. Use your trekking poles for stability and to test the depth of the water when needed.

Keep in mind that water levels in streams can be much higher than normal after significant rainfall, and water levels are often lower in the morning in streams fed by snowmelt or glaciers. To avoid getting knocked down by the pressure from currents, look for slow moving water and avoid bends in streams and rivers.

Be sure to check downstream for potential hazards in case you fall, such as a waterfall, logs or debris in the water. If you end up needing to swim, a submerged log could pin you down.

Trail Courtesies

It's easy to take the trails that we hike on for granted, but they require a lot of work to maintain by trail maintenance crews, and also by volunteers who are giving back by devoting their time to trails. To reduce the amount of work that must be done, stay on the trail while hiking and don't create new paths or cut-throughs.

It can be tempting to cut a switchback in order to walk a bit less. But keep in mind that switchbacks are created to protect steep areas from erosion. Areas in need of rehabilitation may be marked closed with signage, or rangers may place tree limbs or rocks across a side trail to discourage use. Respect these closures to assist with the restoration process.

Generally speaking, dry grass is more resistant to trampling than other vegetation. Wildflower meadows are fragile and walking through them should be avoided. When going off-trail, avoid hiking in single file. Have your group spread out to reduce the impact and lessen the chance of creating a new user trail.

BE RESPECTFUL

Give others space on the trail and yield to other hikers who may need to pass you. When hiking in a group, don't take up the whole width of the trail, and don't block the trail when taking a break. Keep noise such as yelling to minimum. Use headphones if you like to hike with music. In general, be respectful.

While on the trail keep in mind that people enjoy using the outdoors in many different ways. The Pacific Northwest has a wealth of hikers, backpackers, equestrians, ATV riders, and mountain bikers. When encountering horses or pack animals, step off trail and quietly wait for them to pass.

Some trails have restrictions on use. Be aware of these constraints. For example, do not hike on a mountain bike only trail. Your actions on the trail affect other users, and it's important to minimize those impacts.

Mountain goat in the Enchantments

WILDLIFE

Good trail etiquette also requires that you be respectful to wildlife. Many visitors to the backcountry make the venture each year in order to experience wildlife. Your chances of spotting wild animals will be better if you keep noises to a minimum while hiking. While observing animals, it is vital to limit interactions and not approach them. Humans can be stressful and, at times, harmful to the creatures that we wish to enjoy. In most cases you will want to remain quiet and make slow movements when encountering wildlife. Even if they appear sick or wounded, never touch an animal.

Bears are the exception to the rule of being quiet. When traveling in bear country, it is beneficial to make some noise to avoid surprising a bear. Startled bears can be dangerous bears. Backpackers in bear habitat will sometimes travel with a bell, clap as they walk, or simply let out a "hey bear" every few minutes. The most common bear that backpackers may encounter in the Pacific Northwest is the black bear. Black bears are solitary creatures that typically avoid humans. Fatal black bear attacks are extremely rare, but should you encounter a bear, stand your ground and make noise. Most black bears will retreat. Be especially cautious around bear cubs. The mother bear is likely not far away and will be defensive of her cubs.

Dogs need to follow trail etiquette too!

PETS

When bringing your pet on a backpacking trip, it is your responsibility to keep them under control and limit their impact. Remember that everyone is on the trail to enjoy the experience, and not everyone enjoys other people's pets. Don't allow them to approach other hikers and/or their pets without permission. Keep them out of other camper's tents and gear, and away from food preparation areas. They should not chase or disturb wildlife, or dig and do damage to trails, campsites, or cultural sites.

As a pet owner, you will need to deal with your animal's waste. It is a misconception that their waste is better for the environment than human waste. Know when and where they need to go, and either pack it out or bury it, applying the same guidelines as for human waste. If using doggie bags, don't leave them beside the trail. Even if you intend to pick them up on the way out, it detracts from the wilderness experience for others to see litter alongside the trail.

Navigation

It is extremely important to take navigational gear with you on each trip. Some of the most tragic stories revolve around those who got lost just a short ways off of well traveled trails and never made it back. The two most basic instruments that any backpacker needs are paper maps of the entire area to be traveled and a compass.

MAPS

Store maps in a ziplock or waterproof map bag to keep them dry. Topographic maps are the map of choice for most backpackers. This type of map allows the navigator to decipher land features using contour lines and elevation markers.

See the Trip Planning Section on page 34 for more info on map options.

USING A COMPASS

A map is always more accurate when used in conjunction with a compass. The baseplate compass with the ability to adjust the declination is recommended for those learning to navigate. A more advanced feature is a sighting mirror, which allows you to find a more precise line of travel in the backcountry. Whatever compass you decide upon, avoid gimmicky compasses that can be found on novelty items such as keychains or zippers. These are not properly calibrated for navigation.

ELECTRONIC NAVIGATION TOOLS

GPS units and phone navigation are useful tools for navigation, but always carry a paper map as a backup since batteries can die and technology can encounter unexpected issues leaving you without a navigation aid.

Gaia (gaiagps.com) is one of the best navigation apps for smartphones. With it, you can track where you are on the trail, add waypoints for your camp location, water source, or any places you want to remember later, as well as view stats on your hike after it's completed.

When using an app to track your hikes, check it against your paper map on a regular basis so you'll know where you are in case your electronic device fails. This also helps in learning how to read a paper map. Look at the paper map first and try to calculate your location, then check the app for confirmation.

Using the Gaia GPS app for navigation on trail

LEARN TO USE NAVIGATION TOOLS BEFORE A TRIP

Of course, all of these tools are worthless unless you have a working knowledge of how to use them. Don't wait until your trip to build your map and compass skills. Classes, books, and even YouTube (check out the free video series by Columbia Orienteering) are all good resources for learning. If using a smartphone app, download the app and any maps needed, then learn the features you plan to use before you hit the trail.

How to Pack a Backpack

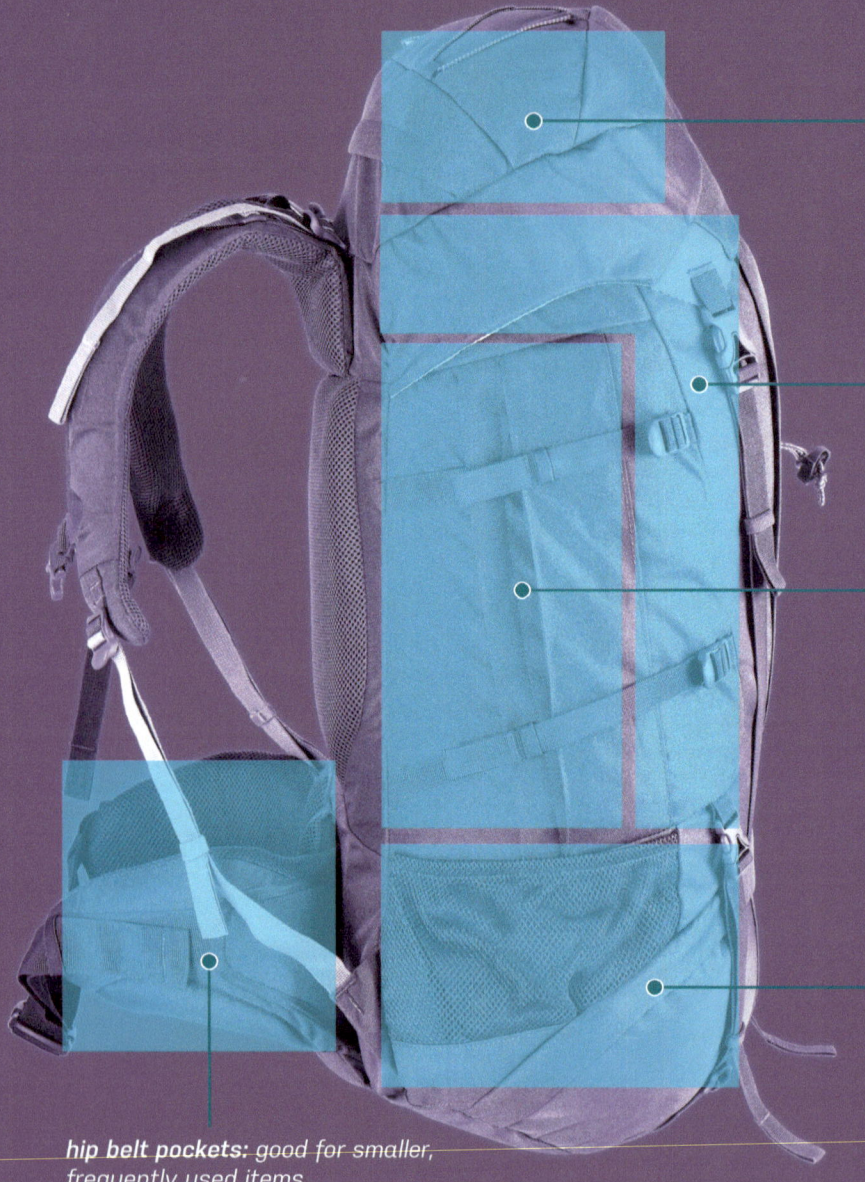

top lid: *items that may be needed during a hike*

main compartment, outer & top: *medium and lightweight items*

main compartment, closest to the back center: *heaviest items*

main compartment, bottom: *lightweight bulky items*

hip belt pockets: *good for smaller, frequently used items*

There's no one way to pack a backpack. Instead, practice loading until you find a method that works best for you. A well loaded backpack will feel balanced and won't shift around when hiking, providing stability on trail.

PACKING A BACKPACK

To get started, lay out all of your gear and separate based on when you'll use items. For example, items not used until you are at camp are usually kept in the bottom and middle of the main compartment of a pack and more frequently used items that may be needed while hiking are kept at the top of a pack and in external pockets.

In general, it's a good idea to have as much inside the pack and pockets as possible, with fewer items attached or hanging on the outside. This will help prevent snagging or scraping gear on branches or rocks, and will make the load more stable.

When loading a pack, stack items in rows (like a row of bricks or a stack of cordwood) instead of standing items upright. Fill gaps with smaller items such as clothing to make the load solid and stable. The final step is to tighten all compression straps to bring the load in and prevent shifting.

Hydration sleeve or pocket: if using a water reservoir, put this in your pack first since it will be difficult to do so after the pack is loaded.

Pack liner: if using a pack liner such as a trash compactor bag, place this in the main compartment before loading your pack.

Bottom of the pack: items used at camp, such as sleeping bag, pillow, and extra clothing. Filling the bottom of a pack with lighter bulky items keeps the pack from pulling down and provides a bit of shock absorption.

Center of the pack, closest to your back: your heaviest items, such as water, cook kits, and food, will need to go as close to the center of the pack as possible and as close to your spine as you can get them. Loading a pack with the weight centered and close to you will help with stability and keep it from sagging down or feeling tippy.

Outer and top sections of main compartment: medium and lightweight items such as sleeping pads, tent body, footprint or rainfly, and extra layers.

Top lid: use for items that you may need during your hike. This space is a great place to hold snacks and essentials such as navigation tools and a rain jacket.

External pockets: items that you may need while hiking, including a bathroom kit, water filter, or first aid kit.

Side pockets: for holding water bottles or awkward items such as tent poles, using the compression straps to secure them in place.

Hip belt pockets: good for smaller, frequently used items, such as snacks, a map, sunscreen or insect repellent.

Using liquid fuel? Make sure it's sealed tightly and place at the bottom of the pack (stored below food), or use an external water bottle pocket.

GETTING A PACK ON

Getting a fully loaded backpack from the ground to your back can sometimes be a challenge. Practice at home so it's easier when you're on trail.

1. Begin by loosening the hip belt strap, shoulder straps, and load-lifter straps.

2. Grab the hoist strap (the webbing loop at the top of the pack) with one hand and the harness with the other hand.

3. Stand in a wide position with both knees slightly bent, slide the pack up one leg to your knee.

4. Use your knee or thigh as a shelf to hold the pack in position.

5. While still holding the hoist strap, slip your free arm into the shoulder strap.

6. Using gravity to stabilize the pack while bending slightly forward, place your remaining arm through the shoulder straps.

7. While still bent over, buckle and cinch the hip belt.

8. Stand up and cinch down the shoulders straps, then the load lifter straps (above the shoulder straps), and finally, buckle the sternum strap across your chest.

9. To take off a heavy pack, loosen all of the straps, then do the above steps in reverse.

Basic First Aid

Illness and injury can happen in the backcountry. Not everyone can be a doctor, but everyone can have the knowledge to use items found within a first aid kit to treat common ailments and injuries.

It is the responsibility of every backpacker to take care of themselves and communicate any concerns to their group. Safety is imperative on trail, and there is no shame in ending a trip early to obtain proper care for an illness or injury.

This section will address injuries and illnesses that more commonly affect backpackers. It will also focus on how they can be treated if the issues are minor. The individual may need to be evacuated for further medical attention should the problem be severe. This chapter is not meant to be a replacement for in-person medical training.

Taking a wilderness first aid class is highly recommended for anyone who backpacks on a regular basis. Classes can be found through organizations such as the Red Cross, National Outdoor Leadership School (NOLS), and Recreational Equipment, Inc (REI).

BLISTERS

More times than not, the first sign of a blister will be a "hot spot." These are described as red, sensitive areas that are, well, hot. You can save yourself a great deal of pain by treating all hot spots before they turn into a blister. It's common for hikers to allow blisters to form because they don't want to stop the group's progress. Hot spots are truly a case of "a stitch in time saves nine" because care is usually easy. Blisters, at their best, can be an annoyance. At worst, they can prevent an individual from hiking, and they may even cause an emergency situation.

Healing hot spots caused by friction can be easy. The goal of treatment is to stop friction from occurring. Many times irritation can be reduced by switching out warm, damp socks with a fresh non-cotton pair. Clean any debris such as rocks or sand out of your boots. Tighten your boots so that they are comfortable and provide support. Friction may also be reduced by covering the affected area with sports tape, moleskin, liquid bandage, or duct tape. Yes, duct tape does fix everything!

If your sore spots do turn into blisters, there are long-standing debates about how it should be handled. Popping a blister could, quite literally, open your foot to the dangers of infection.

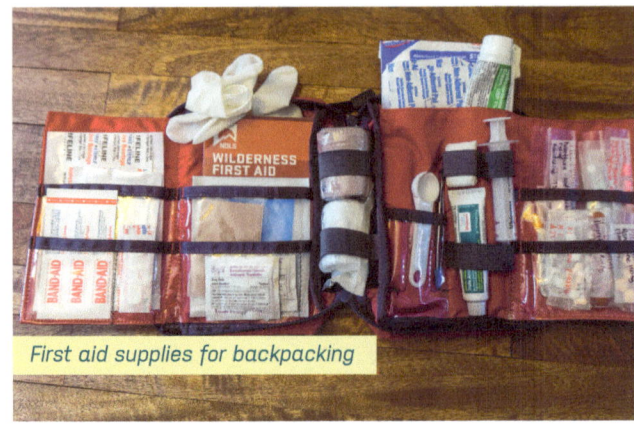

First aid supplies for backpacking

But there are times that popping a blister might be necessary. For example, if you can't get a boot back on without lancing it. Larger blisters may be prone to open on their own. In these situations it would be better to pierce it in a clean, sterile way rather than in a dirty sock. Hikers must use their best judgement to decide what is the preferred choice in their situation.

To proceed without popping, first clean the affected area with soapy water or antiseptic wipes. Padded bandages such as moleskin or foam may be cut into a donut to protect the blister. Use a few layers of the padded bandage if the swelling is severe. The idea is to have the bandage raised higher than the blister. Next, use a piece of non-adhesive gauze or a gel pad as a layer over the top. This will prevent the final layer of adhesive tape from tearing skin. Good old duct tape or medical tape will work to hold this all together. If you have any benzoin tincture, it can be added as an adhesive to make moleskin or tape more sticky. Do note that benzoin is also an antiseptic, and it will burn for a few moments if the skin is broken.

Should you choose to pop a blister, make the process as sterile as possible. Clean the area with soapy water or wipes, then lance the blister with a sharp object such as a needle. Sterilize the needle by heating it over a flame, such as a lighter, until it is red hot. Alternately, you may apply alcohol to the needle if you have it available in your first aid kit. Once the needle is both sterile and cool, use it to prick a small hole in the blister. Drain the fluid and wipe with a sterile gauze. Do not remove the loose skin over the blister as that will increase chances of infection. Apply antibiotic ointment to the site and apply a padded bandage.

BURNS

The two most common forms of burns in the backcountry are sunburns and burns from hot liquids. Like most first aid topics, prevention is key.

To prevent sunburn, apply sunscreen regularly and wear protective gear such as hats and SPF rated clothing. Areas with snow or water can reflect sun rays and increase exposure. Sun exposure can be more severe in high elevation. Be sure to take additional precautions in these regions.

Take extra care when cooking. Always set stoves on a stable, level surface to prevent a pot of boiling water toppling over. While using a stove, be ready to jump out of the way quickly should the stove or pot topple over.

If you do become burned, by the sun or otherwise, you may find relief by applying a wet bandana or cloth to the affected area. If possible, run cool and clean water over the burn for 10-15 minutes. Many first aid kits contain an analgesic (painkilling) gel that may be topically applied to the skin. The affected area should be cleaned, especially if blistered, to prevent infection. Cover the area with a sterile gauze bandage. Some people may find relief from swelling and pain by taking over-the-counter pain relievers such as ibuprofen or aspirin.

ABRASIONS

Abrasions, otherwise known as the good old fashioned scratch or scrape, can occur for a variety of reasons. But when it comes down to it, most could be avoided by wearing long sleeves and pants while tromping around on overgrown trails.

Should you end up with a scratch, your first course of action will be to clean the area. Soapy water will usually do the trick. If the cut is deep you may need to use an irrigating syringe and clean water to force any debris from the wound. After the area is cleaned, most abrasions will require little more than antibacterial ointment and an adhesive bandage.

HEAT RELATED ILLNESSES

In warm months, your best option for avoiding a heat related illness is to refrain from hiking during the hottest part of the day. In most regions of the Pacific Northwest this is typically around 3pm. In extreme hot weather, consider starting hikes in the early morning in order to be off trail by the afternoon.

If you find yourself feeling nauseous, dizzy, or having muscle cramps, it could be time to cool off. Heat related illnesses come with an array of symptoms. These may include the previously listed as well as excessive sweating, hot and dry skin, headache, increased heart rate, or confusion. If you or anyone in your group is experiencing heat related illness, the first step is to get to shade. Drinking water is encouraged. If available, use a damp cloth to wet the skin and fan to cool. Do not resume physical activity until all symptoms have passed. Heat illnesses can become life threatening, and it is best to provide care during initial onset.

HYPOTHERMIA

Despite common assumptions, hypothermia (a decreased core body temperature) can occur any time of year. Those backpacking in the Pacific Northwest must be vigilant of hypothermia as the wet climate can make it much harder to stay warm. Key factors to prevention include clothing choice, caloric intake, and keeping your gear dry.

The onset of hypothermia can be subtle and might begin with uncontrollable shivers as the body attempts to warm itself. Some people will lose fine motor skills as hands become numb. As the progression of hypothermia continues, the individual may develop the "umbles," defined as mumbling, stumbling, and fumbling.

For mild to moderate hypothermia, the goal is to warm the individual. Remove them from the elements by setting up a shelter. Add layers of warmth to what they are already wearing. This may include removing any wet gear and wrapping them in a sleeping bag. The person may be warmed through high calorie foods and a warm drink. It's helpful if the warm drink is high in calories, such as hot chocolate, but if that isn't available, try hot water. You may also use an external heat source such as a fire, chemical heat packs, or another warm body to bring up the hypothermic person's core temperature.

FIRST AID INFO

Some first aid kits come with a small instructional booklet. While it may seem like unnecessary weight, when an emergency situation happens, you'll be happy to have that information to get you through it. Smartphone apps for first aid are another option. Many of these apps can be used offline at times when you don't have cell service.

Choosing a Campsite

Finding a suitable campsite can make the difference between getting a good night's sleep, or tossing and turning most of the night. Where you set up camp also can have impacts on the natural environment, so it's good to be aware of a few guidelines.

CAMPSITE SELECTION

Whenever possible, camp at already established sites rather than creating a new one. These can often be identified by areas void of vegetation. Look for a spot with bare ground or gravel, or a smooth ledge of rock, and avoid pitching a tent on sensitive vegetation. The damage from being trampled by a tent can take years to recover. Never pitch your tent in fragile areas such as wildflower meadows.

In high-use areas, you may be required to camp at designated campsites marked with signage in order to help reduce the impact that so many people visiting a place can have. Contact an area's ranger station to learn more about campsite requirements, including the need for advance reservations or permits.

Locating your campsite near a water supply will make it easier to get water for cooking and cleaning without needing to carry a larger quantity of water a long distance. Just be sure to set up camp at least 200 feet away (about 70 steps) from streams, rivers, and lakes to enable wildlife unhindered access to water sources, and to protect the fragile environment near the water's edge.

Attempt to find an area off the trail, out of view, and away from other campers so that all parties can enjoy the solitude.

Factors that may improve the conditions of your campsite location include:

+ Avoid low spots and drainage areas that may fill with water when it rains.
+ Stands of trees can provide shelter from the wind, are usually warmer than exposed areas, and can help to prevent condensation from morning dew.
+ In high winds, look for a location with boulders, shrubs, or trees that can provide a windbreak.
+ If insects are present, try finding a more exposed and breezy area that might help to blow them away.
+ In hot weather, find a spot with at least partial shade to avoid sweltering inside your tent, but also to prevent damaging the fabric of your tent from exposure to direct sunlight for prolonged periods.

- Colder air settles in low-level areas such as valleys, canyons, and beside water sources, so set up camp in a sheltered area on higher ground in cold weather.
- For sleeping comfort, find a flat area to pitch your tent to avoid rolling downhill all night long. If you have no choice but to sleep on a bit of a slope, keep your head uphill.
- When camping on a beach, make sure to set up well above the high tide line.

DISPOSE OF WASTE PROPERLY

Keeping a clean and organized camp enhances the wilderness experience for everyone, and helps to prevent wildlife from raiding your camp. A major part of keeping a clean camp is disposing of waste properly. You've likely heard the adage of "pack it in, pack it out." The idea of leaving nothing behind is an important piece of land ethics. It can be easy to leave small bits of trash behind. Before you leave a campsite, walk through to ensure that all trash, including small bits of plastic or food waste such as nut or seed shells are removed.

DON'T ALTER THE LANDSCAPE

Always, always leave things how you found them so that others may enjoy the beauty of the wilderness. Do not create new fire rings, lean-tos, or other "improvements." If you move rocks to create a better space for your tent or kitchen, replace them when you are done. Trees should be left as they are and not altered. Even the act of placing a nail in a tree can open it to disease.

LEAVE IT WHERE YOU FIND IT

While backpacking you may have the opportunity to find cultural artifacts and other natural objects such as feathers, rocks, arrowheads, or antlers. These types of objects are essential to the wilderness experience. By leaving these items, you are allowing fellow backpackers the opportunity to have the same sense of wonder and discovery that you experienced upon finding them. Should that not be enough motivation to leave items where you found them, there are several laws, such as the Archeological Resources Protection Act of 1979, which forbids the removal of these types of objects in many areas.

> Learn more about low impact backpacking practices in the **Leave No Trace Seven Principles** section on pages 40-41.

Camp Kitchens

For meal preparation while backpacking, a separate kitchen location should be selected when possible. Kitchens serve the purpose of keeping food smells confined to a single area, and help to prevent animals, big and small, from being attracted to your sleeping location.

preparing dinner in the backcountry

A designated camp kitchen in the North Cascades

LOCATION OF CAMP KITCHEN

Backcountry kitchens and food storage areas should be set up no closer than 200 feet (about 70 steps) from water sources, and preferably at least 200 feet from your sleep area when possible. This is especially important in bear country. Many established campsites already have a place set up for cooking, with a fire ring and rocks or logs placed for sitting. If you need to create a camp kitchen area, an ideal location is on a durable surface such as bare ground or on rocks to help protect the surrounding environment.

FOOD PREPARATION

While heating your backcountry cuisine, be sure to place your stove on a level surface. Flat rocks work best when available. Many backcountry injuries result from a pot of boiling water falling off an unstable stove and burning the user. Follow the stove manufacturer's instructions to avoid accidental fires, fuel spillage, and other potential issues. And don't cook in your tent – using a stove in an enclosed area can put you in danger of both a fire and carbon monoxide poisoning.

CLEAN UP

All camp kitchen trash should be packed out. To cut down on the amount of packaging and food waste on trips, **prepare at home** by bringing properly sized meal portions, eliminating excess packaging materials, and repackaging foods sold in bulky bags or boxes. Food packaging should not be burned in a campfire due to the coatings on most packaging.

Washing dishes: Dish cleaning should be done away from water sources. If you choose to use soap for cleaning, use biodegradable soap. While it is a common belief that biodegradable soap can safely be used in streams, lakes, and other water sources, that is not true. Even biodegradable soap can increase nitrogen levels and negatively impact aquatic life.

After cleaning your dishes, strain out any food scraps (natural materials like sticks, leaves, or moss can be helpful in this process). The remaining waste water should be spread out over a wide area and away from water sources, never in them. Food scraps should be packed out, not buried, to prevent wildlife from learning to get food from areas where humans camp, and to prevent them from damaging an area to access buried food.

PROPER FOOD STORAGE

If you don't store your food properly, you may attract wildlife to your campsite. Keeping food in a tent or on the ground near the tent is not recommended. Most people think of protecting food from bears, but small critters can be especially troublesome and will gnaw through backpacks and tents to get to food. Just like a camp kitchen, your food storage area should be away from camp, preferably at least 200 feet when possible.

HOW TO HANG A FOOD BAG USING THE PCT METHOD

Food hanging kit: 25 feet of cording/rope, a stick (or tent pole repair part), carabiner, small rock sack.

Place rocks in the small stuff sack and attach to the carabiner. Choose a branch at least 10 feet off the ground and sturdy enough to hold your food bag. Throw the rock sack over the branch. Take the remaining section of rope and pull through the middle of the carabiner.

Remove the rock sack from the carabiner. Clip your food bag to the carabiner and raise by pulling the end of the rope until the food bag is up against the branch.

Reach up as high as you can and tie the stick or pole repair part to the line using a clove hitch knot.

Raise the stick, which lowers the food bag at the same time until the stick acts as a stopper, preventing the food bag from coming down any farther. Leave the remaining cording hanging freely. There's no need to tie it off with this method.

To access your food bag, pull on the hanging cord to bring the stick down. Remove the stick and then let the line bring the food bag down low enough to retrieve.

Hanging food: Most places will require food to be hung. In bear country, the hang will need to be 15 feet off the ground and 8 feet away from the base of the tree. In areas where bears aren't an issue it is still necessary to do a critter hang, which can be at a lower height. Pans used for cooking food, bowls, plates, mugs and utensils should all be hung with your food since they will likely hold onto food smells even after washing.

Bear protection: In some backcountry locations, such as national parks, bear canisters may be required for storage of food, trash, and scented items. Some ranger stations loan or rent bear canisters in areas where they are required. While bears may be able to retrieve and move a bear canister, they will not be able to get inside. Don't keep the canister in your tent. Instead, store it away from your campsite. Be careful about leaving it in a place where it could roll off a cliff or into a stream if knocked around by curious wildlife or clumsy campers. *See the Food Storage section on page 19 for more info about food storage gear options.*

Some backcountry campsites have tall poles or wire pulley systems for hanging food, or metal food lockers for communal food storage. These are more common in heavy-use areas where bears are accustomed to looking for food. Be sure to use them when they are available.

Hydration & Filtering Water

The human body is 60% water. As we exercise, we lose some of that water through exertion and sweating, so it's important to stay hydrated and avoid issues related to dehydration.

hydration is essential!

How much should you plan to drink? A general rule of thumb is half a liter of water for every hour of moderate exercise in moderate temperatures. Increase the amount of water needed for increased intensity or in warmer temperatures.

TIPS FOR STAYING HYDRATED

+ Keep water available so it's easier for you to stay hydrated by using a hydration bladder or water bottles that you can reach without stopping to remove your pack.
+ Pre-hydrate on the way to the trailhead or before each day's hike.
+ Remind yourself to drink when it's cold out since your body may not provide the same clues that it needs hydrating as in warmer weather.

REPLACE ELECTROLYTES

When you sweat, your body loses important minerals known as electrolytes, which include sodium, potassium, calcium and magnesium. Even mild electrolyte loss can lead to a decline in performance levels, but significant electrolyte loss can lead to a low sodium level condition known as hyponatremia. For these reasons, it's appropriate to replace electrolytes when needed. Powdered electrolyte replacement drink mixes or tablets are easy to take on trips and mix with water. Another option is to look for electrolyte capsules that contain a similar ratio of minerals as the breakdown found in sweat.

WATER SOURCES

Be aware of potential water sources prior to setting foot on trail. Review a map of the area and look for lakes, rivers, streams, and the tributaries that drain into them. Smaller tributary streams may not be shown on maps, but look for potential drainage channels at the bottom of ridges.

ACCESS TO WATER

Choose a campsite that has good access to water (but remember to set up camp at least 200 feet from the water source). Leave room for wildlife to access the water, steering clear of setting up camp near obvious animal tracks – which will also help to keep them out of your camp.

collecting water to filter

FILTERING WATER

Plan to treat water with filters, purifiers or chemicals any time that it will be collected from natural sources such as rivers, lakes, or snowmelt. The best water sources for filtering are clear and flowing water, such as streams or pond outlets. If the water is gray and filled with glacial silt, pre-filter for sediment using small piece of fabric such as a bandana so it doesn't clog your filter. Avoid water with algae or thick muddy water. Stagnant or murky water should be your last option.

Food & Nutrition

Your body works hard to get you where you are going while backpacking, so it's important to provide it with enough calories, protein, healthy fats, and other nutrients to sustain you.

NUTRITION

It's essential to understand how the calories you eat fuel your trips since you'll burn more calories during a day of backpacking than on a normal day. How much you burn depends upon your body, the terrain, elevation, pack weight, and distance. And remember, not all calories are equal, so replenish yourself with a diverse mix of foods.

Carbohydrates provide the quickest energy and are the main focus of most backpacking meals. Simple sugar provides a quick energy burst, but grains, vegetables, beans and legumes provide complex carbs that supply longer-lasting energy. Protein sources, such as meat, eggs, dairy, whole grains, and legumes, are good for renewing muscles and body tissue. And healthy fats from nut butters, olive oil, or coconut oil can provide slow-burning energy needed by backpackers.

MEAL PLANNING

The key to meal planning for backpacking is to bring food that is calorie dense and lightweight. Your food also needs to be appealing to eat, because it's not uncommon to experience a loss of appetite when you're tired from exertion. A good rule of thumb on how much food to bring is 1.5 to 2 pounds of food per day. Where you fall in that range depends upon your size and energy output.

Breakfast: Your hiking style will largely influence your breakfast choices. Trail bars and dry smoothie mixes are good options for a no-cook quick start to the day. Instant oatmeal is a backcountry standard that's easily enhanced by adding freeze-dried fruits and nuts or seeds. A more traditional breakfast might include powdered eggs, bacon jerky, or hash browns served with instant coffee or tea.

Lunch is typically eaten while taking a short break on trail, often without the use of a stove. Calorie dense items like dried fruits, nuts, jerky, cheese and crackers are good options.

Dinner recharges your batteries at the end of a long day. Whether you plan to use a packaged meal that only needs water to prepare, or a meal that includes a bit more effort to cook, plan on dinner being the largest meal of the day.

Sorting food into rows for each day of a trip

Hot drinks like coffee and tea can provide needed warmth and a mental lift as well as a boost of energy.

MEAL OPTIONS

Most backpacking meals will consist of commercial packaged meals, home made dehydrated meals, or meals you assemble using dried ingredients. All are great options, and your choice may come down to cost and convenience.

Commercial freeze-dried or dehydrated packaged meals are the most convenient but they're also expensive. Outdoor retailers carry these types of meals, and the market is expanding greatly, providing options for organic, gluten-free, vegetarian and vegan diets. Additionally, grocery stores can be a source for dried foods such as pasta, rice, and soup mixes, or instant mashed potatoes.

Dehydrate your own meals. Unless you'll be using these right away, seal tightly and store in a freezer until ready to use.

Assemble meals using dried ingredients. You can purchase freeze-dried or dehydrated ingredients (or dehydrate your own) and combine to make a meal.

Fresh food can boost the nutrition of meals. Options that tend to hold up well without refrigeration include apples, avocado, cabbage, and hard cheeses.

CONVENIENCE

Many people prefer meals that are prepared simply by adding boiling water to a package and eating directly from the bag after the food is fully rehydrated. Cooking in a pan is another option that many find to be a more enjoyable dining experience. While it will be necessary to do a small amount of clean up, advantages are not having to eat from a plastic bag, and not adding a smelly, messy food bag to your camp trash.

The Backcountry Bathroom

One of the biggest fears for new backpackers is how to deal with going to the bathroom in the backcountry. There's really nothing to fear, but before you go, learn how to lessen your impact on the local ecosystem following these guidelines.

PEEING IN THE BACKCOUNTRY

Look for a spot with privacy, and away from water, campsites, or trails. To avoid damaging sensitive vegetation, look for areas with bare ground or rocks whenever possible.

Ladies! There's no reason to use toilet paper when peeing in the backcountry. Toilet paper left behind is unsightly, ruining the wilderness experience for others, plus it takes a very long time to decompose. Instead, consider one of these methods:

+ Use a pee cloth. A bandana works well for this purpose. Tie it to the outside of your pack to dry and the sun will help to sanitize it. Wash it as needed.
+ Add a spritz of water from a traveling bidet, then dry with a clean cloth.
+ The drip dry method works for some people. Do a quick shake after peeing.
+ Female urination devices are funnels shaped to fit up against the body so women can stand to pee. These devices can take some time to get used to, so practice at home in your shower.
+ Use natural materials such as the long side of a smooth stick, leaves, moss, or a smooth rock.
+ If you must use toilet paper, pack it out.

POOPING IN THE BACKCOUNTRY

If you poop in the woods, will anyone be able to find it? Far too often, the answer is yes. Too many people are irresponsible and leave their waste under rocks, in shallow uncovered holes, or worse, right in a campsite. Don't be that person. Learn the proper methods for dealing with human waste.

In most areas of the Pacific Northwest, you should bury your waste by digging a cathole at least 200 feet away (about 70 steps) from any water source, including seasonal watersheds such as sandy washes. It is also ideal if it is at least 200 feet

Backcountry bathroom kit

away from your campsite. As a general rule of thumb, catholes should be dug progressively farther away from camp the longer you are staying at a site or the more people that you have at that site.

To dig and use a proper cathole:

+ Look for a spot that has loose, organic soil and, if possible, some sunlight. Both will help to speed up the decomposition process.
+ Remove the top layer of duff above the soil and set aside.
+ Using a camp trowel can make digging a lot easier, but some people use sticks, rocks, or even trekking poles.
+ Dig a hole at least 4 inches wide and 6-8 inches deep.
+ Squat over the hole and do your business.
+ Consider using a bidet to spray water for extra cleaning and reducing the amount of toilet paper needed.
+ Wipe with toilet paper, wipes, or natural materials (make sure to pack out all toilet paper and/or wipes).
+ Cover the hole using the soil you dug out. Tamp it down, then replace the duff layer, placing a small branch or two over the spot to discourage critters from digging it up.
+ Clean your hands with sanitizer.

PACKING OUT TOILET PAPER

It's better for natural ecosystems if you pack out toilet paper. Bathroom tissue will decompose eventually but in most environments it will take at least five months. In more arid environments it could be months longer. To pack out toilet paper, use double layers of plastic bags or use odor-proof bags.

To disguise the contents, use a solid color doggie bag to hold the toilet paper and place that inside another plastic bag.

USE A BIDET

There's nothing like a blast of water to make you feel clean and refreshed! Bidets have been used in homes for a long time, but traveling bidets are easy to take on trips. A traveling bidet is simply a container with a spray head that's filled with water. Just place it in position and squeeze to spray after using the bathroom. You may not even have a need for toilet paper after using a bidet. Just keep in mind that you will need an ample source of water for filling the container.

MENSTRUATION PRODUCTS

Like toilet paper, feminine hygiene products should be carried out, never buried or burned. Some women prefer to use a menstrual cup to eliminate the amount of waste that must be packed out.

See the Toiletries section on page 25 for more info about supplies for bathroom kits.

Backcountry composting toilet in the North Cascades

BACKCOUNTRY TOILETS

Some backcountry areas, especially those with heavy use, have pit toilets located near campsites. It is always best for the surrounding ecosystem to use these privies when they are available. Please remember that others on the trail make use of the same facility. If you make a mess, clean it up. Always close the door or lid if there is one, as it will help keep flies and other critters out. And pack out your toilet paper. Someone has to haul the human waste out of these outhouses, either by helicopter or mule, and you will be doing them a favor by reducing the refuse thrown into them.

PACKING OUT HUMAN WASTE

In heavy-use, sensitive or high elevation areas, you may be required to pack out solid human waste. Don't worry, there are products made to assist with this task! Toilet waste kits available for purchase often contain additives such as odor neutralizers and gels for absorbing liquids, and some include toilet paper and hand sanitizers. You can also make your own at home with re-sealable plastic bags (odor proof bags would be a good choice here!) and kitty litter. Whether purchased or homemade, the concept is simple. Do your business in the bag and pack it out.

Personal Hygiene

You don't have to be dirty and smelly on a backpacking trip. Say goodbye to at least some of the funk with these personal hygiene tips:

- Establish a daily ritual of washing your body after hiking each day to wipe away sweat, dirt, sunscreen, and/or insect repellant. A simple sponge bath in your tent can be done with wipes, or with water and a small pack towel.
- Do camp laundry using a re-sealable plastic bag filled with water. Wring out as much moisture as you can and lay wet items in a sunny spot to dry.
- If using soap, use unscented biodegradable soap and distribute dirty water on dirt or rocks, never in or near a water source.
- Bring hand sanitizer and scrub your hands every time after using the bathroom and before preparing meals. Soap and water also work well.
- Brush and/or floss your teeth at least once every day.
- Bring separate base layers just for sleeping in.
- Keep your feet clean and dry to avoid problems with bacteria. Wash your socks each day and change to a clean pair before going to bed.
- Take a dip in a stream, pond, lake or river. Make sure to wipe off sunscreen and insect repellent before getting in. The chemicals used in these products (even those containing natural ingredients) can harm the ecosystems in water sources.

Campfires

Having a campfire is often synonymous with camping, but before you build a campfire, consider the potential wildfire danger as well as the impact on the local environment.

When considering whether or not to have a campfire on a backpacking trip, there are several questions to ask:

Are fires allowed where you'll be backpacking?

Fires may be prohibited in some areas, including above tree line or in heavy-use areas where wood is scarce, near bodies of water, or in the desert. Check with the ranger station to find out if there are any fire restrictions for your location.

What is the current fire danger level?

Wildfire season in the Pacific Northwest typically peaks in July, August and September with conditions changing on a regular basis, so check before a trip to see if there is an elevated fire risk. Even if allowed, consider whether or not a fire is necessary, especially in wildfire season.

Is there enough supply of downed and dry wood for a campfire?

Dead trees are an important part of the forest ecosystem, providing decomposing wood that nourishes the soil and provides life to wildlife, yet many heavy-use areas have been completely stripped of dead wood. Look around to see how much is available to collect when making a decision about having a campfire.

BUILD A LOW IMPACT CAMPFIRE

Remember the Four D's when collecting firewood: dead, down, detached, and diameter. The wood that you collect should always come from a dead source. Never cut limbs off of a live tree. Even if the source is dead, it should have already fallen down. Before removing limbs from downed trees, collect limbs that are already detached from trees. Finally, the diameter of logs being burnt should be no thicker than your wrist. Larger timber is a challenge to burn completely down to ash and leaves scarred wood behind.

Use an existing fire ring whenever possible. If an established fire ring is not available, your next best options are to create a mound fire or use a fire pan.

Use an existing fire ring for a campfire

Fire mounds can be built upon a thick layer of mineral soil – sandy, light-colored, nonfertile dirt, often found in streambeds, gravel bars, or in uprooted tree holes. Spread mineral soil in a circle about 18 to 24 inches in diameter and 6-8 inches deep. Build the fire on top of the mound. Disperse the mound when you are finished.

Fire pans are exactly what they sound like: pans with sides at least three inches high on which a fire is built. Best practice is to raise the fire pan onto rocks or mineral soil so as to avoid scorching the earth.

FIRE BUILDING TIPS

To build a campfire, you'll need to collect tinder, kindling, and firewood. Tinder can be natural materials found around the campsite such as wood shavings, small twigs, or dry leaves. After wet weather, finding dry tinder can be difficult, so consider bringing fire starter from home. Inexpensive and lightweight options include dryer lint or cotton balls soaked in alcohol or coated with vaseline. Larger twigs and small branches less than 1 inch in diameter make good kindling.

Start with the tinder as the bottom layer and build a teepee or log cabin shape with the kindling. Oxygen is important for a long lasting fire, so leave spaces in the structure for air flow. Light the tinder, and as the fire burns the kindling and increases in strength, add a few smaller pieces of firewood. Once the fire is going strong, add larger pieces of firewood a few at a time.

FIRE SAFETY

Fires should be kept under control at all times. While it may be tempting to create a bonfire that reaches to the stars, flames no more than a few inches high will do in most situations and will be much easier to control.

Never leave a campfire unattended. Before going to bed or leaving camp, scatter the coals around in the fire ring and **douse the fire completely with water**. Stir the ashes and add more water if needed. Ashes should be cool to the touch.

In order to make clean up easier, let the wood burn completely to ash when possible. Pack out trash instead of burning it in a fire. Most food packaging is coated with plastic or foil and can't be completely burned in a fire.

Campfire at Shi Shi Beach

CLEAN UP

Even when using an existing fire ring, cleaning up after a campfire is an important part of low impact practices.

After a fire is completely out, any remaining large chunks of charcoal should be crushed into smaller pieces. This can be done by using using a stick or rock. The ash can then be thinly scattered in a broad area away from your campsite. Be aware that some river corridors in the Pacific Northwest may not allow for the scattering of ashes in order to protect the water supply. In this case ashes should be carried out.

TIPS FOR STAYING WARM AT NIGHT

+ Go to bed warm. Don't wait until you get cold to head to your tent for the night.

+ When purchasing a sleeping bag, keep in mind that the temperature ratings are relative and don't consider individual cold intolerances. If you tend to sleep cold, get the warmest bag you can afford. For some people, a 20 degree bag works fine even in the winter, and for others, a 0 degree bag is needed to stay warm year round.

+ Get a sleeping bag that fits you. A bag that is too large has to work harder to heat up the empty space. Women-specific sleeping bags usually have more insulation in the footbox and hips.

+ If your sleeping bag isn't keeping you warm enough, you probably need a sleeping pad with more insulation.

+ In freezing temps, use a closed-cell foam pad with your air mattress for an extra layer of insulation.

+ Fill a hard plastic water bottle with hot water, making sure it's tightly sealed, cover with a sock or clothing, then place in your sleeping bag and hold between your thighs to warm up.

+ Eat high fat food like peanut butter just before going to bed.

+ Drink a cup of hot herbal tea or hot cocoa before bed.

+ About 15 minutes before going to bed, place a few hand warmers in your sleeping bag.

+ Looser layers are better than tight layers, which constrict blood flow.

+ Wear a hat to cover your head when sleeping.

+ Change into clean, dry clothes and socks when setting up camp or before getting into your sleeping bag.

+ Do a few jumping jacks before going to bed, being careful to not break a sweat or you'll end up with damp base layers.

+ Wake up cold? Do a few push-ups in your tent.

+ Have to pee? Your body will transfer body warmth to a full bladder, so don't wait to get up and empty it.

Gear Maintenance

Spend a few minutes after each trip to clean your gear and make any needed repairs. Outdoor retailers carry products specifically for cleaning, repairing, and waterproofing various types of gear, clothing, and footwear. Always follow manufacturer guidelines when caring for your gear.

TENTS

To clean a tent, never use a washing machine or dryer as both can damage the materials. Using water and a sponge to spot clean is often sufficient. For heavier duty cleaning, fill a bathtub with cold to lukewarm water and swish it around gently and hang to dry. Avoid using household cleaners or detergents as they may damage the finish on a tent's fabric. For mold, mildew, or a lingering odor, use an enzyme cleaner before permanent damage or stains set in. Leaky seams can be repaired with brush-on seam sealer, and spray-on products can replenish the waterproof finish on the tent exterior or rain fly.

Tents should be completely dry when stored. It may not always be possible to dry your tent while on trail. If this is the case, set it up or hang it to dry at home. Store tents loosely in a cool, dry location.

SLEEPING BAGS

After each trip, unzip and air out your sleeping bag, making sure it's completely dry before storing. Sweat, dirt, and skin oils can damage the insulating properties of a sleeping bag, so keep it clean to prolong the lifespan. Most of the time, all that is needed is a spot cleaning. To do this, use a small amount of non-detergent cleaner with a toothbrush, concentrating on areas where skin oils tend to accumulate such as the hood and draft collar. To rinse, hold the outer layer away from the insulation to keep from getting the inside wet.

For a full washing, follow the manufacturer's instructions and use gentle cleaning products made for down or synthetic-filled gear. Or, consider using a professional laundering service.

Contact outdoor retailers to locate a laundry service in your area. If washing at home, use a front-loading washing machine. The agitators in top-loading machines can damage zippers and seams. Drying can take a long time, especially for down bags. Use a tennis ball or dryer balls to help increase the loft of the insulation.

Small tears in the fabric can be repaired with adhesive patches. To fix a zipper, try cleaning it with a brush and lubricating the teeth with a product made for zippers. If that doesn't work, contact the manufacturer or locate a repair shop that specializes in outdoor gear.

Sleeping bags should not be compressed when stored as this will decrease the loft. Store in a large breathable bag, or hang in a dry area.

SLEEPING PADS

Sleeping pads can be cleaned with warm, soapy water and a sponge. Hang to dry and store flat or loosely folded with the valve open.

BACKPACKS

The best way to care for a backpack is to spot clean the dirty area immediately. Washing may become necessary because spot cleaning may not always solve the issue. Handwash a backpack in a large tub filled with lukewarm water and use gentle detergent. A soft brush and some elbow grease will go a long way when taking care of heavily soiled spots. Once the backpack is sufficiently clean, refill the tub with clear, cool water and rinse to remove all suds. Hang to dry with all pockets open and lubricate zippers if needed.

WATER BOTTLES AND HYDRATION BLADDERS

To keep water bottles and hydration bladders clean, wash them after each trip and allow to completely dry before sealing and storing. To clean, use a diluted bleach solution or soapy water and rinse thoroughly. To fully dry a hydration bladder, prop it open with a small item to allow air in. Keep zip closures and screw tops open until completely dry.

Giving Forward

As hikers and backpackers in the Pacific Northwest, it's easy to take the wilderness areas that we spend time in for granted. But we need to help protect and maintain these areas if we want them to survive over time. *If we lose them, they are gone forever.*

One way you can make a positive difference is to support non-profit environmental and trail-related organizations that are doing work on our behalf. Becoming a member is a good way to support them. Additionally, many of these organizations offer volunteer opportunities, advocacy involvement, group hikes, and stewardship programs.

HERE ARE A FEW ORGANIZATIONS TO CONSIDER SUPPORTING:

+ Washington Trails Association (wta.org)
+ Trailkeepers of Oregon (trailkeepersoforegon.org)
+ Friends of the Columbia River Gorge (gorgefriends.org)
+ Oregon Wild (oregonwild.org)
+ Pacific Crest Trail Association (pcta.org)
+ Pacific Northwest Trail Association (pnt.org)
+ Oregon Natural Desert Association (onda.org)
+ Klamath-Siskiyou Wildlands Center (kswild.org)
+ Wilderness Society (wilderness.org)
+ American Hiking Society (americanhiking.org)
+ Sierra Club (sierraclub.org)
+ Audubon Society (audubon.org)
+ Nature Conservancy (nature.org)

PHOTO CREDIT: HELEN GROSS

Backpacking Trips

1 SOUTHWEST WASHINGTON
Siouxon Creek

2 OREGON COAST
Tillamook Head

3 COLUMBIA RIVER GORGE
Wahtum Lake

4 EAGLE CAP WILDERNESS
Wallowas Lakes Basin

5 GOAT ROCKS WILDERNESS
Snowgrass Flat

6 THREE SISTERS WILDERNESS
Green Lakes

7 MOUNT ADAMS WILDERNESS
Killen Creek

8 MOUNT HOOD WILDERNESS
Cairn Basin

9 MOUNT HOOD WILDERNESS
Burnt Lake

10 INDIAN HEAVEN WILDERNESS
Deep Lake

The backpacking trips in this book are geared to many types of hikers: beginners, those getting back into backpacking after a long hiatus, or anyone who wants an easy to moderate trip to a scenic location.

Many of the trips in this book are to popular areas, some of which tend to be crowded and may require special permits. These destinations are popular for a reason, as they go to some of the most scenic places in the Pacific Northwest on trails that are suitable for beginning backpackers. Many first-timers will take comfort in backpacking in areas where other backpackers, and sometimes park rangers, are relatively nearby. As you build skills as a backpacker, you'll likely find yourself planning trips to less traveled places. Regardless, these trips are a great place to get started.

Due to the impact so many people visiting a place can have on an area's ecosystem, this makes it even more important to follow low impact practices. Whenever possible, visit these areas during the week and plan to arrive early in order to get a campsite.

The maps in the book have been created for planning purposes. See the map section on page 34 for more info on where to obtain maps suitable for navigation.

Southwest Washington: Siouxon Creek

The trail beside Siouxon Creek passes several stunning waterfalls as it travels through an old-growth forest lush with many shades of green: deep emerald pools of water, ferns, mosses and lichens, and towering conifers.

This trip is suitable for everything from a quick one night trip to a multi-day exploration of everything this area has to offer. Set up a basecamp in one of many established creekside campsites and then choose day hikes, ranging from easy to strenuous.

THE HIKE IN

From the parking lot, take a short side trail to Siouxon Trail #130. Turn right, and head downhill, crossing West Creek on a super-sized wood bridge. Just after the bridge, an open section of campsites sits between the trail and creek, but it's only 0.25 miles from the parking lot, so keep hiking. There are plenty of campsites ahead, and all of them have a view of the creek or a waterfall.

Nearly every surface in the forest is covered in moss and lichens. The forest floor is littered with "nurse" logs, fallen trees that decay and provide nourishment to the forest, often with new trees rooting over them. At 1.0 miles is a junction on the right with the Horseshoe Ridge trail. Continue past this on the main Siouxon Trail.

At 1.5 miles in is **Horsetail Creek Falls** (57 ft.), a fan-shaped waterfall that spills down black basalt rock in three tiers. A small bridge crosses the creek above the waterfall. Continue for 0.1 miles past the bridge to a side trail that leads to three good campsites, one of which has a great view of the waterfall. Access to the creek is not easy here, but there is a small tributary stream another 0.1 miles ahead on the main trail from the campsite trail junction. Continue on the main trail for another 0.25 miles to **Siouxon Falls** (28 ft.), a thundering cataract waterfall with a wide bowl-shaped deep pool. A large campsite is located here on the opposite side of the trail from the waterfall viewpoint. To get a view of the top of Siouxon Falls, go past the waterfall to a side trail on the left.

Continue on the main trail, skirting above the creek and through boggy lower sections of forest. At 3 miles from the trailhead, several campsites are located next to the creek. Set up camp in this area for the best creek access. If all of these sites are taken, additional campsites are about a mile ahead, off the Chinook Creek Trail. Cross a small stream on logs and boards placed over a wide section of rock and turn left at the trail junction, crossing a bridge over Siouxon Creek. One campsite is immediately to the left, with several more a short distance ahead and to the right.

Photos, left to right from top: Siouxon Creek; Siouxon Falls; Horseshoe Falls; typical section of heavily forested trail.

TRIP PLAN

TRAILHEAD: Siouxon Trail #130

TRAILHEAD GPS COORDINATES: 45.94652, -122.17780

TRAILHEAD ELEVATION: 1,335 ft.

HIKE TYPE: basecamp with day hikes

HIKE IN TO CAMPSITES: 3 miles

ELEVATION GAIN: 525 ft.

EXPOSURE: forested

TYPICALLY OPEN: March - Nov. (contact ranger station for current conditions)

BEST TIME: April - June

WATER ACCESS: Siouxon Creek and tributary creeks

DOGS ALLOWED: yes

CAMPFIRES: check for current restrictions

MAPS: USGS: Siouxon Peak, Bare Mountain; Green Trails: Lookout Mountain

FEES/PERMITS: NW Forest Pass may be required beginning in 2021, check with the ranger station

CONTACT

Gifford Pinchot National Forest
Mount Adams Ranger District
2455 Hwy 141
Trout Lake, WA 98650
(509) 395-3400

Photos, left to right from top: fern-filled section of trail; Chinook Falls; campsite next to Siouxon Creek; Wildcat Falls; Horseshoe Falls.

DAY HIKES FROM CAMP

The distance and elevation gain for each of these options is from points indicated on the map, not from the trailhead.

14-MILE FALLS & CHINOOK FALLS
2 miles round trip, 275 ft. gain (from the Wildcat trail junction)

From camp, continue on the Siouxon Creek trail for 0.7 mile to a small stream crossing on logs and boards placed over a wide section of rock and turn left onto the Chinook Creek Trail 130-A, crossing a bridge over Siouxon Creek. **14-Mile Falls** can be accessed at the end of the bridge by turning right and carefully following the rock around to the left. This is an ideal location for relaxing next to the waterfall. To reach Chinook Falls, continue on the Chinook Creek Trail for 0.3 miles, passing campsites on the right. When you reach Chinook Creek, stay to the right and go up and over a small rocky knob to **Chinook Falls** (62 ft.). In early spring, the creek may be too high to reach the falls, but if not, you can step down the rocky wall to the water's edge. Return the same way back to camp.

WILDCAT FALLS + CHINOOK FALLS LOOP
2.2 miles round trip, 985 ft. gain (from the Wildcat trail junction)

This loop hike requires fording streams three times, best done when water levels are lower in late summer and fall. Earlier in the season, the water levels are much higher and potentially difficult to cross safely. Located 3.0 miles from the trailhead, the trail junction for Wildcat Falls is easily missed. Look for the Wildcat Trail sign posted high on a tree on the left side of the trail. Turn left, passing a small campsite, and continue to the water's edge. If it is safe to cross, ford the creek and pick up the trail on the opposite side. Follow signs for the Wildcat Trail, heading steadily uphill beside the creek before making several switchbacks to a viewpoint of the lower of three segments of **Wildcat Falls** (125 ft.). Continue for 0.2 miles to a viewpoint closer to the top of the waterfall. Turn around at this point and head back to Wildcat Creek near the point at which it flows into Siouxon Creek. Ford Wildcat Creek and pick up the trail on the other side at a sign for Chinook Trail #130-A. Continue on the Chinook Trail for 0.5 miles to Chinook Creek. This section of trail is sometimes brushy and faint, but easy to follow. Ford Chinook Creek at **Chinook Falls** (62 ft.) and pick up the trail on the other side. Pass several campsites and cross a bridge to a trail junction with Siouxon Creek Trail #130. Just to the left is **14-Mile Falls**, with a deep pool of water to cool off in during hot weather. At the trail junction, turn right on the main Siouxon Trail. Continue for 0.7 miles to the Wildcat Trail junction to complete this loop hike.

UPPER SIOUXON CREEK TRAIL
3.4 miles round trip, 330 ft. gain (from the Wildcat trail junction)

Begin this hike at the junction with the Chinook Trail, approximately 4 miles from the trailhead. Instead of turning and crossing the bridge, stay on the main Siouxon Trail. Pass a view of **14-Mile Falls** and continue on this less traveled section of trail as it climbs high above Siouxon Creek. In about 0.5 miles is a partial view of **Middle Siouxon Falls** (37 ft.). The trail continues beside the creek, eventually descending to a wide rocky section next to the creek. Continue to **Upper Siouxon Falls** (16 ft.), and then for another 0.5 miles to a good stopping point just before the trail requires a ford of Calamity Creek. Head back the same way.

DRIVING DIRECTIONS TO TRAILHEAD

From Portland, drive east on I-84 for 5.7 miles to Exit 8 for I-205 North.

Continue on I-205 for 7.8 miles, crossing the Columbia River and entering Washington.

Take the Highway 500 Exit 30A, 30B and 30C, then stay to the left for 30B Highway 500 E.

Continue for 26.2 miles, driving through Battle Ground where Highway 500 becomes Highway 503.

Just after the town of Amboy, turn right to stay on Highway 503.

Just past the Mount St. Helens National Monument Headquarters, turn right on NE Healy Road.

Set your odometer at each of the following segments because the roads are unmarked.

Continue on NE Healy Road, which becomes Forest Road 54, for 9.2 miles to a fork, turning left on FR 57.

Continue on FR 57 for 1.2 miles, turning left on FR 5701.

Continue on FR 5701 for 3.7 miles to the parking area just before the road ends.

DRIVE TIME/DISTANCE FROM PORTLAND
1 hour 40 minutes; 55 miles

ROAD CONDITIONS
Although mostly paved, some of the Forest Roads are rough with potholes. While suitable for most vehicles, higher clearance vehicles are recommended.

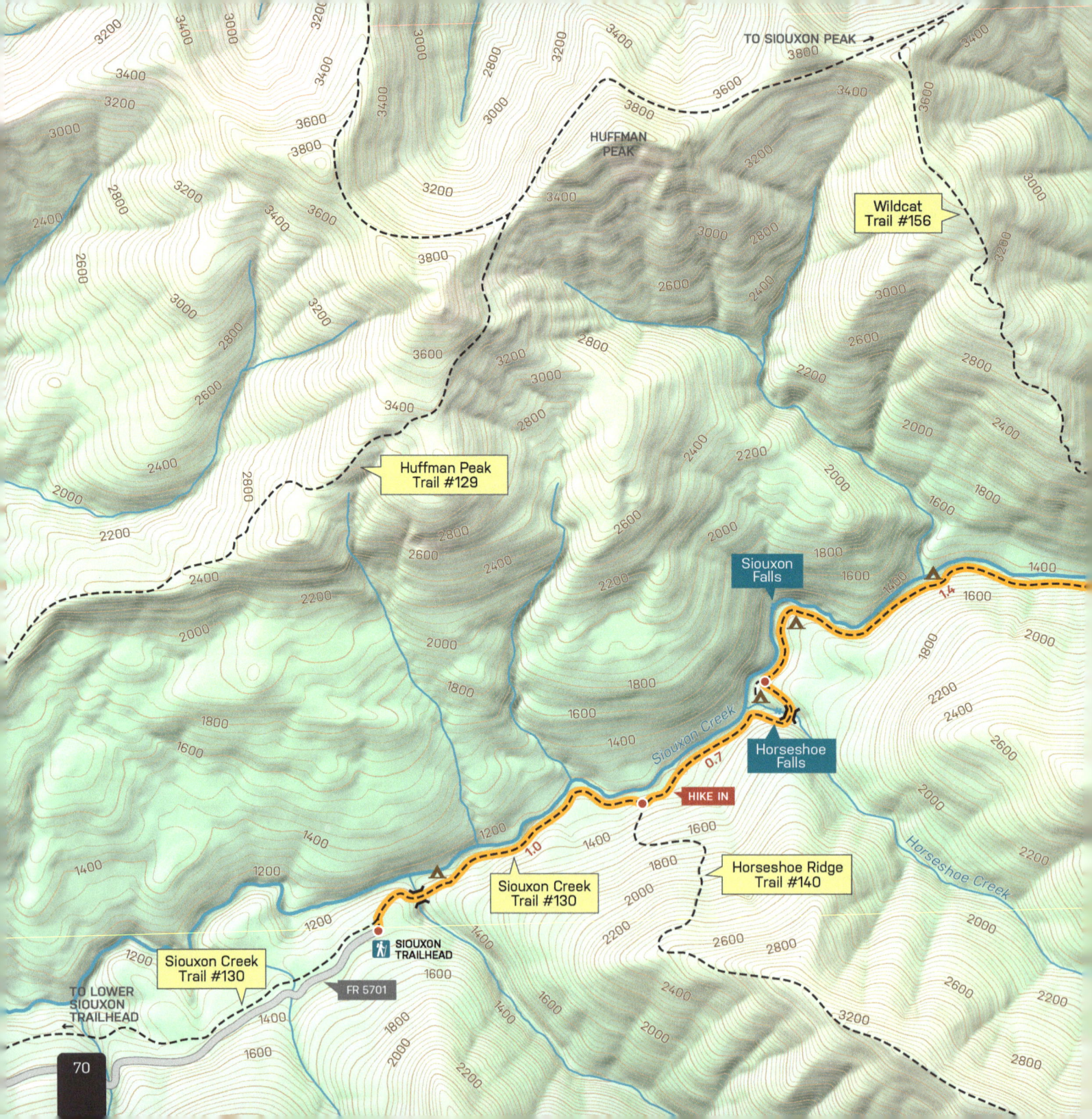

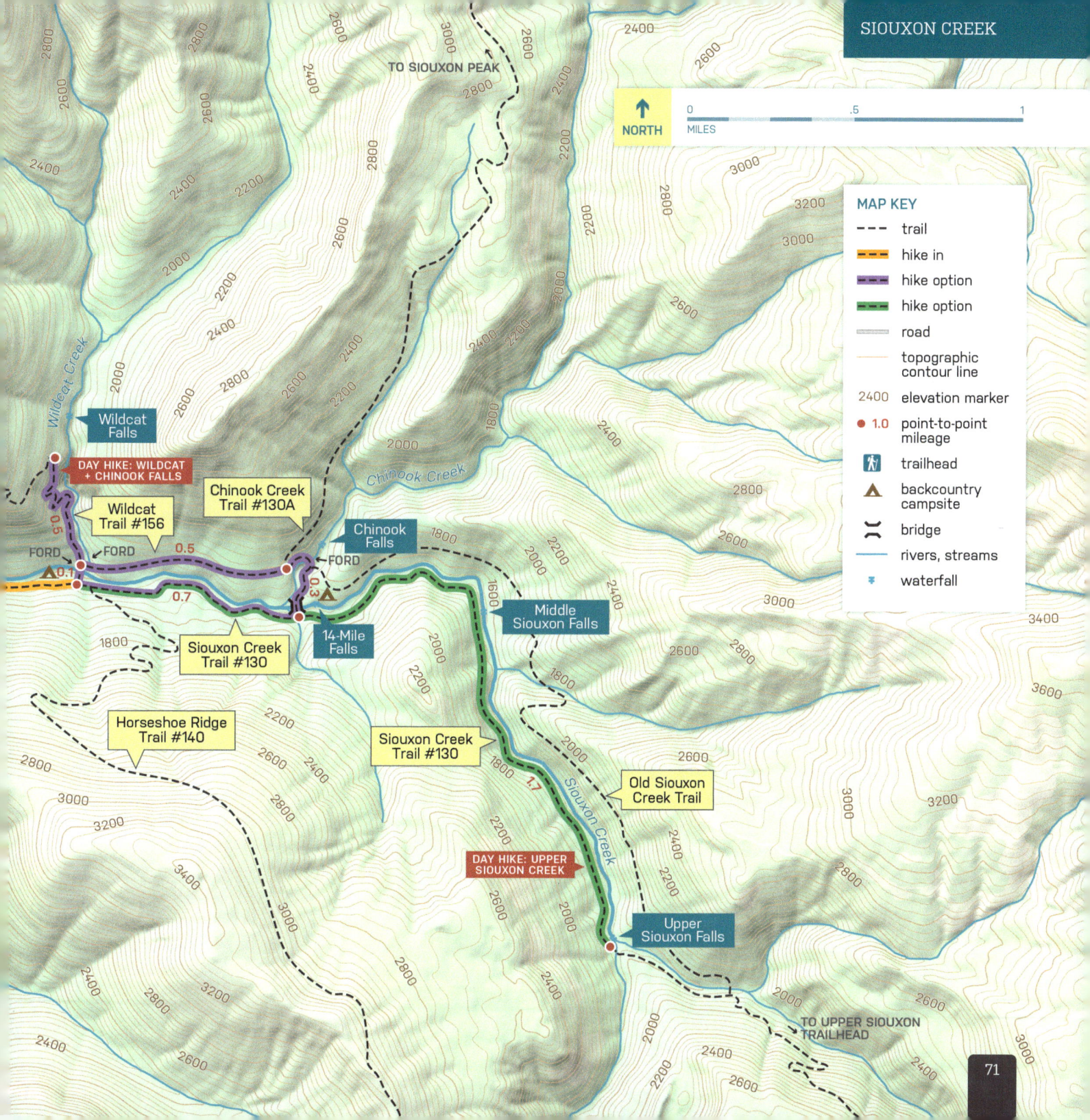

Oregon Coast: Tillamook Head

Follow a section of the Oregon Coast Trail through temperate coastal rainforest across Tillamook Head to a hiker camp high above the ocean.

Located in Ecola State Park between the towns of Seaside and Cannon Beach, the hiker camp on Tillamook Head is one of the few established backpacking campsites on the Oregon Coast.

THE HIKE IN

This historically significant trail in Ecola State Park played a part in the Lewis and Clark expedition in 1906. Members of their group crossed the headland to buy whale blubber from the Native Americans in what is now Cannon Beach. The name Ecola originates from the Chinook tribe's word for whale: "ekoli."

Begin the hike at the Tillamook Head trailhead in Seaside. The first section of trail heads through a thick undergrowth of ferns and berry shrubs, and then switchbacks up, with most of the elevation gain happening in the first mile.

The remaining three miles are generally level, with only occasional glimpses of the ocean. Large segments of the trail are frequently very muddy and often have downed trees to climb under or over. This dense forest is filled with Sitka spruce, largest of all spruce trees and native to the west coast. The last segment of trail descends via several short switchbacks before reaching the hiker camp.

The hiker camp has three wooden shelters and a large area behind them to set up tents. Unusual features for a backpacking site include a vault toilet (no cathole digging!), and bundles of firewood to burn in the campfire ring are often available to purchase. There's even a covered shelter with a picnic table. What there isn't, however, is access to water... unless you hike another 1.5 miles down the trail (see the Clapsop Loop to Indian Beach day hike on page 75) to Indian Creek.

From the hiker camp, a short sidetrail leads to a viewpoint of Tillamook Lighthouse, passing by an old World War II bunker formerly used to house radar equipment.

Photos, left to right from top: wood shelters at the hiker camp on Tillamook Head; Tillamook Head trailhead in Seaside; tent area behind wood shelters at the hiker camp.

TRIP PLAN

TRAILHEAD: Tillamook Head

TRAILHEAD GPS COORDINATES: 45.97241996, -123.958397

TRAILHEAD ELEVATION: 250 ft.

HIKE TYPE: basecamp with day hikes

HIKE IN TO CAMPSITES: 4 miles

ELEVATION GAIN: 1,250 ft.

EXPOSURE: forested

TYPICALLY OPEN: all year (contact ranger station for current conditions)

BEST TIME: July - Sept.

WATER ACCESS: none

DOGS ALLOWED: yes

CAMPFIRES: check for current restrictions; the hiker camp has a fire ring and usually has firewood available for a fee

MAPS: Ecola State Park

FEES/PERMITS: none

CONTACT

Oregon State Parks
Ecola State Park
PO Box 681
Cannon Beach OR 97110
(503) 436-2844

Photos, left to right from top: View from Tillamook Head Trail to Indian Beach; Tillamook Lighthouse from the viewpoint; large sections of the trail are often muddy; World War II bunker; hiking in; fern-filled coastal forest.

DAY HIKES FROM CAMP

The distance and elevation gain for each of these options is from points indicated on the map, not from the trailhead.

CLATSOP LOOP TO INDIAN BEACH
3.0 miles round trip, 800 ft. gain (from the hiker camp)

While the hiker camp on Tillamook Head is perched high above the ocean, it's a relatively short hike to Indian Beach. From the hiker camp, take the Tillamook Head Trail south (1.6 miles) to the parking lot at Indian Beach. This section of trail is usually less muddy than the hike in from Seaside. Views along the way are stunning, with Indian Beach and its many sea stacks, and Indian Point, Cannon Beach and the Coastal Mountains seen through the tall evergreens. A popular destination for surfers and beachgoers, Indian Beach is often crowded during the summer. For an easier hike back, return on the Clatsop Loop Trail (1.4 miles), a former Forest Service road.

INDIAN BEACH TO ECOLA POINT
3 miles round trip, 300 ft. gain (from the Indian Beach parking lot)

From Indian Beach, continue on the Oregon Coast Trail for 1.5 miles through old-growth coastal rainforest. The trail is often muddy, with frequent blowdowns to climb over or around. Regardless, the views along this hike are frequent and well worth the effort, including the wide open expanse of the ocean, Indian Beach, Tillamook Lighthouse, and Tillamook Head. The coast line is ever changing, with erosion making the cliff edges unstable, so use caution and stay behind fences and railings. At Ecola Point's grassy bluff, follow the paved trails to several excellent viewpoints. Bring your binoculars for a chance to see gray whales migrating south in mid-December to mid-January, returning north in late March.

CRESCENT BEACH
2.4 miles round trip, 200 ft. gain (from the Crescent Beach trailhead at Ecola Point)

One of the most photographed beaches in Oregon, this pocket beach is only accessible via the 1.2 mile hike down a steep and often muddy trail, making it less crowded than most beaches on the northern coast. Best done at a low tide, it is possible to do this hike at higher tide, but there will be less beach to explore. At Ecola Point, look for the Crescent Beach trailhead near the restrooms. The trail begins by going up several sections of stairs, then alongside the road for a short distance. Re-enter the forest trail, descending slightly and leading to cliff side views of the ocean and the community of Cannon Beach. The trail is eroding in several places here, with significant drop-offs, so pay attention to children and dogs. The next section of trail is through dense coastal forest, full of Sitka spruce and sword ferns. Cross a small creek on a footbridge and begin a slight ascent. The same creek drops to the beach in a waterfall. After winding through the forest at the highest part of this hike, begin descending to a trail junction. Take the route to the right, which descends to the beach in several steep switchbacks. On the beach, head to the right for the waterfall. At low tide, continue all the way to the end of the beach to access small sea caves.

DRIVING DIRECTIONS TO TRAILHEAD

From Portland, drive 74 miles west on Highway 26.

Take the US 101 North exit (Oregon Coast Highway).

Continue for 3 miles. Turn left at Avenue U.

Continue for 0.2 miles on Avenue U and turn left on Edgewood (which becomes Sunset) for 1.2 miles to the trailhead.

NOTE: Overnight parking is not allowed at the trailhead parking lot. Instead, park at a gravel pullout about 0.2 miles east of the trailhead. There is also no overnight parking allowed at Indian Beach or Ecola Point.

DRIVE TIME/DISTANCE FROM PORTLAND
1 hour 35 minutes; 80 miles

ROAD CONDITIONS
Highway and paved roads all the way to the trailhead.

Columbia River Gorge: Wahtum Lake

With a multitude of trails in the area, Wahtum Lake provides easy access to the high backcountry of the Columbia River Gorge.

Take a short hike in to the primitive campsites on the northwest side of Wahtum Lake for access to several peaks, including Chinidere Mountain, Tomlike Mountain, Green Point Mountain and Indian Mountain.

THE HIKE IN

Wahtum Lake sits at the base of Chinidere Mountain in a glacial cirque — a bowl-shaped basin with steep walls carved by glaciers — and is surrounded by old-growth firs and hemlocks. The Native American meaning of Wahtum is thought to be "lake," so welcome to "Lake Lake."

A small campground is located right at the trailhead, and there are a few designated campsites on the lake shore, but the backpacking campsites are on the northwest end of the lake.

At the trailhead, fill out a wilderness permit, then take the "Wahtum Express," 200 stairs down to the lake, or take the Wahtum Lake Trail for 0.4 miles to the Pacific Crest Trail (PCT). Continue on the PCT for 0.2 miles, then stay to the right at the junction with the Eagle Creek Trail. In another 0.2 miles, look for a sign for Chinidere Mountain at a campsite on the right. There are several campsites in this area, but keep going on the Chinidere Cutoff Trail for the best sites. A short distance ahead, cross the outlet for Wahtum Lake (the beginning of East Fork Eagle Creek) on a log jam. After crossing the lake, head uphill on switchbacks. Several designated campsites are tucked into the trees via short side trails in this area. For access to water for filtering, head back to the lake at the log jam crossing.

Once set up at camp, there are many trails in this area to explore, including Eagle Creek, Herman Creek, the Pacific Crest Trail, Benson Plateau, and Waucoma Ridge.

For a longer backpacking loop, start at Herman Creek or Eagle Creek at the Columbia River. Wahtum Lake is the halfway point for this 33-mile loop.

Note: the 2017 Eagle Creek Fire impacted this area. Check with the ranger station for info on current restrictions or trail closures.

Photos, left to right from top: Wahtum Lake; Chinidere Mountain trail; view of Mount Hood from Chinidere Mountain.

TRIP PLAN

TRAILHEAD: Wahtum Lake

TRAILHEAD GPS COORDINATES: 45.57737, -121.79263

TRAILHEAD ELEVATION: 3,980 ft.

HIKE TYPE: basecamp with day hikes

HIKE IN TO CAMPSITES: about 1 mile

ELEVATION GAIN/LOSS: 75 ft./-360 ft.

EXPOSURE: forested

TYPICALLY OPEN: May - October (contact ranger station for current conditions)

BEST TIME: June - Sept.

WATER ACCESS: Wahtum Lake or tributary streams

DOGS ALLOWED: yes

CAMPFIRES: check for current restrictions

MAPS: USGS: Wahtum Lake; Green Trails: Bonneville Dam

FEES/PERMITS: NW Forest Pass; self-issued wilderness permit at the trailhead

CONTACT

Mount Hood National Forest
Hood River Ranger Station
6780 Highway 35
Parkdale, Oregon 97041
(541) 352-6002

Photos, left to right from top: View to the north from Chinidere Mountain, with Mount St. Helens, Mount Rainier and Mount Adams on the horizon; campsite area near Wahtum Lake; trail junction; Chinidere Cutoff Trail; Tomlike Mountain.

COLUMBIA RIVER GORGE: WAHTUM LAKE

DAY HIKES FROM CAMP

The distance and elevation gain for each of these options is from points indicated on the map, not from the trailhead.

CHINIDERE MOUNTAIN
2.4 miles round trip, 915 ft. gain (from beginning of Chinidere Cutoff Trail)

Chinidere Mountain (4,670 ft.) is named after the last reining chief of the Wasco Native American tribe. From the campsites on the north side of Wahtum Lake, take the steep Chinidere Cutoff Trail for 0.8 miles to the Pacific Crest Trail (PCT) junction. Along the way, cross a couple of small streams and follow an old pipe that used to bring water to the formerly developed campsites. At the junction with the PCT, turn left and in about 500 ft., look for the Chinidere Mountain Trail on the right. Head up the Chinidere Trail, which switchbacks several times and crosses a talus slope before turning for the ascent to the top. Unlike a lot of rocky summits, getting to the top of Chinidere does not require any scrambling skills. The summit is wide and mostly flat, with plenty of room to spread out and soak in the surrounding scenery. Views from the top on a clear day include Mount Hood directly to the south, and Mount St. Helens, Mount Rainier, and Mount Adams to the north. On the east side of the summit, look below for a view of Wahtum Lake.

TOMLIKE MOUNTAIN
5.6 miles round trip, 1,100 ft. gain (from beginning of Chinidere Cutoff Trail)

Tomlike Mountain (4,550 ft.), the high point on Woolly Horn Ridge, is named after George Tomileck Chinidere, the son of Chief Chinidere. Begin this hike near the campsites at the north side of Wahtum Lake on the Chinidere Cutoff Trail. After 0.8 miles, reach a trail junction with the Pacific Crest Trail (PCT). Turn right and in 0.3 miles, the PCT heads right. Continue straight, staying to the left on the Herman Creek Trail. Continue for 1.1 miles through thick forest with an understory of bear grass. Just after passing the Anthill trail junction on the right, look for an unmarked but obvious trail on the left, just before a sharp right turn where the Herman Creek Trail descends towards Mud Lake. On this unmaintained trail to Tomlike Mountain, stay to the right side of the ridge. The trail soon opens to views of the East Fork Herman Creek drainage and Mud Lake below. Continue on the ridge crest, pass through an open area and follow cairns to locate the trail as it heads through thick shrubs and small trees. At the base of Tomlike, scramble up a section of loose rock to a ridge leading to the summit. Take in expansive views that include Mount Hood, Mount St. Helens and Mount Adams before returning the same way back to camp.

DRIVING DIRECTIONS TO TRAILHEAD

From Portland, drive east on I-84 for 61 miles to Exit 64 / Hood River / Highway 35.

Turn right at the highway exit, following signs for Government Camp / Mount Hood.

In 0.3 miles, at a four-way junction, continue straight on Highway 35.

Continue for 5 miles, then turn right on Ehrck Hill Drive.

After 1 mile, follow a sharp left turn to continue on Ehrck Hill Drive.

Continue for another 0.3 miles, then turn right to to continue on Ehrck Hill Drive.

After 0.5 miles, continue straight at a four-way junction. The road changes names to Summit Drive.

Continue on Summit Drive for 2 miles to a junction with Dee Highway 281.

Turn left onto Dee Highway and continue for 4.1 miles.

Turn right at Lost Lake Road, then stay to the left after 0.2 miles to continue on Lost Lake Road.

In 1.3 miles, turn left to continue on Lost Lake Road.

In 0.5 miles, turn right to continue on Lost Lake Road.

In 3.1 miles, turn right on FR 13 / Wahtum Lake.

Continue on FR 13 for 4.3 miles.

Turn right on FR 1310 / Wahtum Lake.

Continue for 6 miles to the trailhead.

DRIVE TIME/DISTANCE FROM PORTLAND
2 hours; 90 miles

ROAD CONDITIONS
Paved all the way.

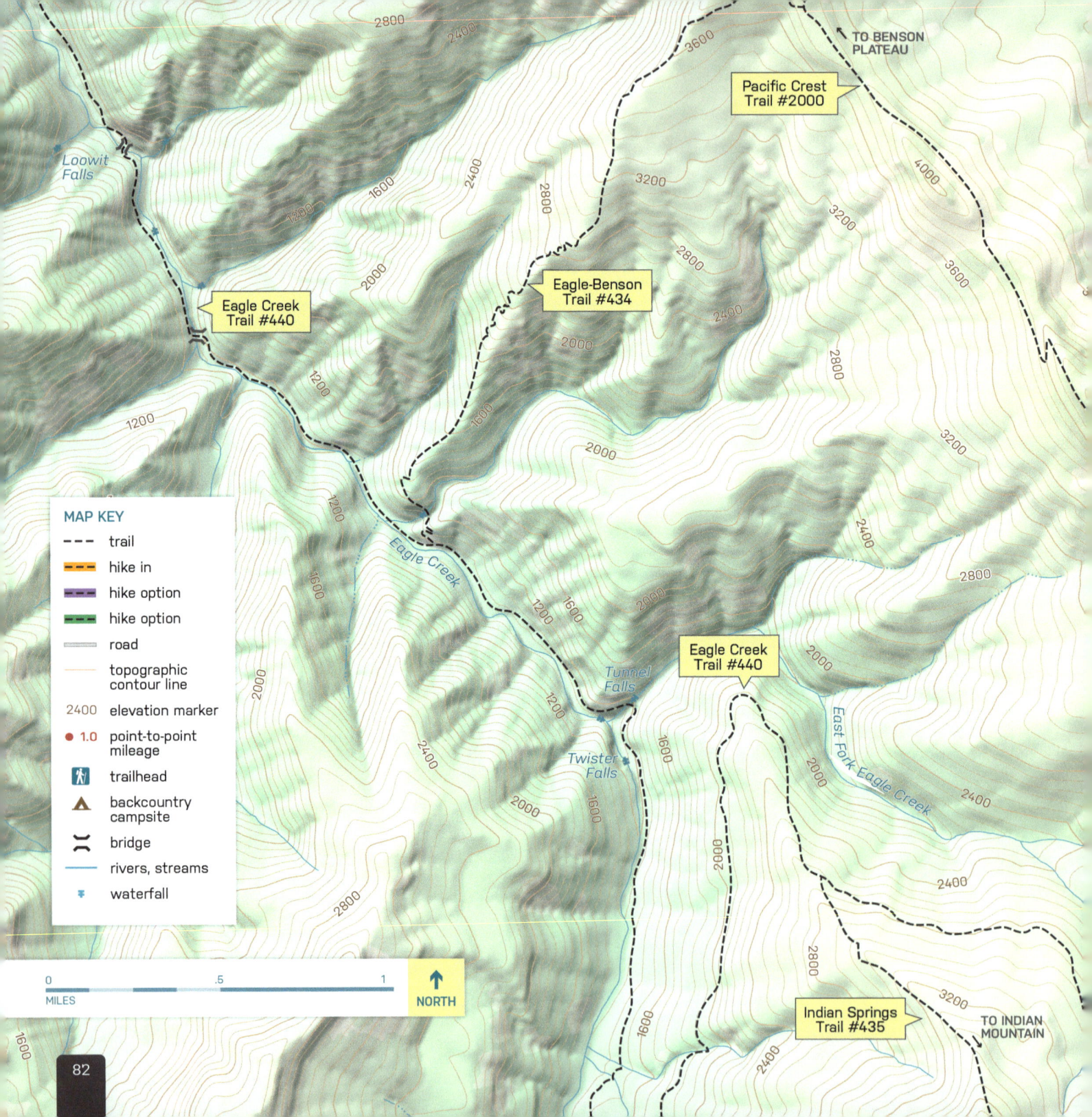

Eagle Cap Wilderness: Wallowas Lakes Basin

Known as the "Alps of Oregon," the Wallowa Mountains are located in Northeastern Oregon, with over 360,000 acres designated as the Eagle Cap Wilderness.

Plan a three or four day backpacking trip to the popular Lake Basin area in the Wallowas and camp near Mirror Lake. Multiple options exist for longer hikes, including to the summit of Eagle Cap Mountain, or over Glacier Pass to Glacier Lake.

THE HIKE IN

The Wallowa (pronounced Wul-OW-wuh) Mountains contain 31 peaks that rise above 9,000 feet, with U-shaped valleys up to a mile below bare granite peaks and ridges. The Lakes Basin is scenery packed – with granite slabs, alpine lakes and meadows scattered throughout and surrounded by peaks.

The Two Pan trailhead (5,600 ft.) provides the most direct access into the Eagle Cap Wilderness. Fill out a free wilderness permit at the trailhead (groups are limited to 12, including stock animals, except in the Lake Basin, where groups are limited to 6). This area is very popular and can be crowded during the summer, so arriving mid-week is highly recommended.

To reach Mirror Lake in the Lakes Basin, the hike in is 7.3 miles with 2,000 ft. gain. After a long drive to reach the trailhead, an easier option is to hike in 3 to 4 miles with approximately 1,500 ft. gain and camp at Lostine Meadows, then hike the remainder to the Lakes Basin the next morning.

From the trailhead, follow the trail a short distance to a junction and stay left, taking the East Fork Lostine River Trail #1662. Cross the East Lostine River on a small bridge, and continue through a forest with Douglas fir, lodgepole pine, and spruce. After the first mile, the route steepens and climbs 11 switchbacks over the next mile, with scenic views to the north.

At about 3 miles in, enter the Lostine Meadow area, with views of Eagle Cap in the distance. The meadows continue for about two miles, with several places to camp in forested areas next to the meadows. Be sure to set up camp on a durable surface, staying off the fragile meadows as much as possible.

Near the end of the meadows, cross a small bridge and begin a gradual ascent for two more miles to a trail junction near Mirror Lake. Continue on the Lakes Basin Trail to Mirror Lake. Numerous campsites are dispersed throughout this area, so take some time to explore and find the best site for your group. Camping within 100 feet of lakes and 100 feet of posted wetlands is prohibited. Campfires are prohibited within 1/4 mile of the lakes in the Lakes Basin.

Photos, left to right from top: view of the Lakes Basin from the Glacier Pass Trail; footbridge on the East Fork Lostine River Trail; Mirror Lake and Eagle Cap.

TRIP PLAN

TRAILHEAD: Two Pan

TRAILHEAD GPS COORDINATES: 45.250219, -117.376395

TRAILHEAD ELEVATION: 5,600 ft.

HIKE TYPE: basecamp with day hikes

HIKE IN TO LOSTINE MEADOWS: 3.2 miles

ELEVATION GAIN: 1,400 ft.

HIKE IN TO MIRROR LAKE: 7.3 miles

ELEVATION GAIN: 2,000 ft.

EXPOSURE: forested at lower elevation; open and more exposed at higher elevation

TYPICALLY OPEN: mid-July - Sept. (contact ranger station for current conditions)

BEST TIME: August

WATER ACCESS: lakes and streams

DOGS ALLOWED: yes

CAMPFIRES: prohibited within 1/4 mile of lakes in the Lakes Basin

MAPS: USGS: Eagle Cap; Green Trails: 475SX Wallowa Mountains

FEES/PERMITS: NW Forest Pass; self-issued wilderness permit at the trailhead

CONTACT

Wallowa-Whitman National Forest
Eagle Cap Wilderness Office
201 E 2nd / PO Box 905
Joseph, OR 97846
(541) 426-5546
(541) 426-4978

Photos, left to right from top: Glacier Lake; outlet of Glacier Lake; Two Pan trailhead; hiking to the Lakes Basin from Lostine Meadows; sunset view of the Lakes Basin, with Matterhorn in the top left and Moccasin Lake on the right.

DAY HIKES FROM CAMP

The distance and elevation gain for each of these options is from points indicated on the map, not from the trailhead.

LAKE BASIN LOOP
5.2 miles round trip, 750 ft. gain (from Lake Basin Trail #1810A)

Beginning at Mirror Lake, take the Lake Basin Alternate Trail #1810A for a counter-clockwise loop through the Lake Basin. On the way to Moccasin Lake, the trail loses about 120 feet of elevation. Several side trails lead to good views of Moccasin Lake and the high ridge above it. Continue past Moccasin Lake to Douglas Lake, losing another 140 feet of elevation. At a trail junction at the east end of Douglas Lake, turn left at the Lake Basin Trail #1810. The trail travels along the north side of Douglas Lake, passing by tiny Craig Lake, then Crescent Lake. There are several nice campsites at the west end of Douglas Lake. Past Crescent Lake, the trail begins an ascent, with several switchbacks and 350 feet of elevation gain up to a junction with the Hurricane Creek Trail #1807. Stay to the left, continuing on the Lake Basin Trail. Along this section of trail, watch for views of the Matterhorn and its 3,000 ft. face of white marble. Pass through several meadow areas and after about a mile, arrive at Sunshine Lake, a small lake with great views of Eagle Cap. Continue on the trail 0.2 miles back to Mirror Lake.

GLACIER LAKE
6.6 miles round trip, 1,800 ft. gain (from Lake Basin Trail #1810A)

Beginning at Mirror Lake, head east on the Lakes Basin Trail for 0.6 miles to the Glacier Lake Trail junction at Moccasin Lake. Rock hop across a small isthmus that separates two parts of the lake, then pass several campsites on a small peninsula. After Moccasin Lake, the trail crosses a small meadow before beginning switchbacks to head up to Glacier Pass. On the way up, take in superb panoramic views of the Lakes Basin area. A small creek runs down a narrow drainage area next to the trail, providing a nice sound of water cascading. Nearing the pass, the terrain is more open and rocky, pasing through a granite bowl with lingering snowfields. Reach the trail sign for Glacier Pass (8,452 ft.), and soon after, Glacier Lake and the peaks surrounding it come into view. From here, the trail heads down switchbacks for about 600 feet. Glacier Lake is incredibly scenic, with islands dotting the turquoise blue water. The trail continues to the outlet of the lake, which cascades down a rocky ravine and becomes the West Wallowa River. Head back the same way to your camp near Mirror Lake.

EAGLE CAP
6.2 miles round trip, 2,000 ft. gain (from Lake Basin Trail #1810A)

The trail to the summit of Eagle Cap is strenuous and steep, with snow lingering in some years until early August. Beginning at Mirror Lake, head west on the Lakes Basin trail for 0.4 miles to the trail junction for the East Eagle Creek Trail and Ivan Carpenter Pass. After a short distance, continue on the East Eagle Creek Trail for 1 mile to a junction with the Eagle Cap Summit Trail, continuing on the Summit Trail for 1.7 miles through an open alpine ridgeline to the summit of Eagle Cap (9,572 ft.). From the top, take in expansive views of the entire Wallowa Mountains, including Lostine Meadows and Mirror Lake below. Return the same way to camp.

DRIVING DIRECTIONS TO TRAILHEAD

From Portland, take I-84 East for 261 miles to Exit 261 Highway 82 / La Grande.

Turn right and continue on Highway 82, following signs for Wallowa Lake for 71.4 miles to Lostine River Road in the town of Lostine.

Turn right on Lostine River Road and continue for 18 miles to the trailhead.

DRIVE TIME/DISTANCE FROM PORTLAND

5 hours 50 minutes; 330 miles

ROAD CONDITIONS

Highways and paved roads for most of the drive. Gravel road the last 12 miles, suitable for most vehicles.

Goat Rocks Wilderness: Snowgrass Flat

Located between Mount Adams and Mount Rainier, Goat Rocks is a series of rugged ridges and peaks that remain from an eroded volcano that once stood over 12,000 feet.

This trip plan is based on setting up basecamp at an established campsite near the Snowgrass Flat/Lily Basin trail junction, with a day hike to Goat Lake and a loop hike around Snowgrass Flat. Additional hike options include heading north on the PCT to the summit of Old Snowy Mountain or south to Cispus Pass.

THE HIKE IN

This area is very popular and can be crowded during the summer, so arriving mid-week is highly recommended. Snow often lingers until late-July, and can return in September, so check on current conditions before planning a trip.

Goat Rocks Wilderness is carpeted in wildflowers from mid-July through August, and with the wildflowers come hordes of flying insects, so be prepared with plenty of bug protection.

Beginning at the Snowgrass Trailhead, the hike begins in a dense low-level forest. In 0.1 miles, pass a junction with a connector trail that leads to the Berry Patch trailhead. Continue on the Snowgrass Trail for 1.5 miles to a swampy area and a bridged crossing of Goat Creek. Just before the bridge, the trail splits, with the trail to the left for horses. Keep to the right and continue on the Snowgrass Trail as it gently ascends for about half a mile. After this, the trail steepens and occasional views of Goat Rocks begin to appear through the trees. Just over 3.5 miles from the trailhead, reach a junction with the Bypass Trail. Continue straight on the Snowgrass Trail, passing several small meadows and views of Mount Adams before reaching a junction with the Lily Basin Trail, 4.4 miles from the trailhead.

Snowgrass Flat is incredibly scenic, with subalpine meadows filled with wildflowers and expansive views of Goat Rocks, including the high rocky peaks of Old Snowy and Ives Peak. When Mount St. Helens erupted in May 1980, it dumped up to six inches of ash in this area, which is still visible today.

Numerous campsites are available via sidetrails off of Lily Basin Trail, as well as along the Pacific Crest Trail and Bypass Trail. Camping is not allowed in Snowgrass Flat. Check for signage indicating closed areas. Choose a durable surface campsite that has already seen use and don't set up camp in any of the meadows. This alpine area is fragile yet gets heavy use, so take special care to minimize your impact.

Photos, left to right from top: view of Goat Rocks from the Lily Basin trail; section of trail lined with wildflowers; Goat Lake, still covered in ice in early August.

TRIP PLAN

TRAILHEAD: Snowgrass #86

TRAILHEAD GPS COORDINATES: 46.4636, -121.5182

TRAILHEAD ELEVATION: 4,650 ft.

HIKE TYPE: basecamp with day hikes

HIKE IN TO CAMPSITES: 4.4 miles

ELEVATION GAIN: 1,550 ft.

EXPOSURE: forested at lower elevation; open and more exposed at higher elevation

TYPICALLY OPEN: mid-July - Oct. (contact ranger station for current conditions)

BEST TIME: August - September

WATER ACCESS: streams

DOGS ALLOWED: yes

CAMPFIRES: check for current restrictions

MAPS: USGS: Old Snowy, Hamilton Buttes, Walupt Lake; Green Trails: 303S Goat Rocks

FEES/PERMITS: NW Forest Pass; self-issued wilderness permit at the trailhead

CONTACT

Gifford Pinchot National Forest
Cowlitz Valley Ranger Station
10024 US Hwy 12
Randle, WA 98377
(360) 497-1100

Photos, left to right from top: view of Goat Rocks from the Lily Basin trail; campsite near the Lily Basin / Snowgrass Flat trail junction; paintbrush and lupines in bloom; Snowgrass Flat / PCT trail junction; bear grass along the Bypass Trail; taking in the view on the Lily Basin trail.

DAY HIKES FROM CAMP

The distance and elevation gain for each of these options is from points indicated on the map, not from the trailhead.

GOAT LAKE
4.6 miles round trip, 1,000 ft. gain (from Snowgrass/Lily Basin trail junction)

Starting at the junction of the Snowgrass and Lily Basin Trails, take the Lily Basin Trail for 2.3 miles to Goat Lake. The trail winds through subalpine meadows filled with wildflowers, and crosses numerous rock-lined streams before ascending the side of a rocky ridge towards Goat Lake. The alpine lake can still be covered with snow and ice into August, and the trails on the ridge can be snow covered into late July or early August, with potential snow bridges over water crossings making the journey more challenging. If you choose to take a dip in the frigid waters of Goat Lake, please remove all sunscreen and insect repellent to protect this fragile alpine environment. Return the same way back to the camp area.

Add-on hike to Hawkeye Point: For expansive views from one of the high points in Goat Rocks, continue on the Lily Basin Trail past Goat Lake. At 0.8 miles, pass a trail junction with the Goat Ridge Trail. Continue on the Lily Basin Trail for about another 0.5 miles to the top of Goat Ridge. Follow the primitive trail on the ridge to Hawkeye Point (7,431 ft.).

SNOWGRASS/BYPASS LOOP
3.5 miles round trip, 1,000 ft. gain (from Snowgrass/Lily Basin trail junction)

From the Snowgrass/Lily Basin trail junction, take the Snowgrass Trail east towards the towering peaks of Goat Rocks for 0.8 miles to a junction with the Pacific Crest Trail (PCT). Numerous side trails lead to campsites all along this loop hike. As the trail ascends, the landscape becomes rockier and more open, with bigger and bigger views of the Goat Rocks. At the PCT trail junction, turn right and head south for 1 mile to the Bypass Trail junction. This section of the trail descends through equally scenic terrain, filled with wildflowers and bear grass (blooming mid-to-late July). Just after a large talus slope is a junction with the Bypass Trail. Turn right and continue for 1 mile to a junction with the Snowgrass Trail. Head through a section of denser forest, then through meadow after meadow. The Bypass Trail area feels more like a fairyland than the other sections of this loop. There are several campsites in this area. Just after crossing the stream, reach the Snowgrass trail junction. Turn right and return to the Lily Basin trail junction and your campsite.

ADDITIONAL DAY HIKES FROM CAMP AREA

+ **Old Snowy Mountain:** 8 miles round trip, 2,600 ft. gain
+ **Cispus Pass:** 8 miles round trip, 1,800 ft. gain

DRIVING DIRECTIONS TO TRAILHEAD

From Portland, drive north on I-5 for 75 miles to Exit 68 / US 12 / Morton.

Turn right at the highway exit, heading east on Highway 12.

Continue on Highway 12 for 61 miles to FR 21, about 3 miles west of Packwood, WA.

Turn right at FR 21, continuing on the gravel road for 13 miles to FR 2150.

Turn left at FR 2150 and continue for 2.5 miles to FR 2150-040.

Stay to the right at FR 2150-040, then turn right at FR 2150-405 (signed for Snowgrass Flat) to the parking lot loop.

DRIVE TIME/DISTANCE FROM PORTLAND

3 hours 30 minutes; 151 miles

ROAD CONDITIONS

Paved highways, then 20 miles of gravel road with washboards and a few potholes, suitable for most vehicles.

Three Sisters Wilderness: Green Lakes

The Three Sisters Wilderness in Central Oregon has a long volcanic history, much of which is visible today. Nestled between South Sister and Broken Top, the Green Lakes area provides great access to exploring the area.

The Green Lakes area sees heavy use during the summer, especially on weekends, so plan to visit during the week for less crowded conditions. This area is under consideration for requiring special backcountry permits. Check with the local ranger station when planning a trip here. Camping in the Green Lakes area is restricted to designated campsites only and campfires are not allowed.

THE HIKE IN

From the trailhead parking lot, head north on the Green Lakes Trail, crossing a large log bridge in the first quarter mile. The trail travels alongside Fall Creek all the way to the Green Lakes, initially through a forested section with views of the creek and several cascading waterfalls. Catch glimpses of South Sister (10,358 ft.) and Broken Top (9,175 ft.) along the way. Pass through several sections of more open forest and meadows, and cross the creek a couple of times on rail-less bridges.

At two miles in, pass the Moraine Lake Trail junction. Just after this, you'll begin to see an enormous wall of lava known as the Newberry Lava Flow on the opposite side of the creek, filled with large chunks of shiny black obsidian. The trail makes two short switchbacks in a mile-long forested section, then heads back to the creek for the rest of the way, crossing several small tributary streams. During July and August, wildflowers are abundant, especially alongside creeks and in ravines.

A sign for the Green Lakes area indicates the locations of 28 designated campsites near the lakes, with GPS coordinates listed for each. Pass a junction with the Broken Top trail and continue straight for the Green Lakes. Reach heart-shaped South Green Lake first, then the largest Green Lake. North Green Lake is approximately 1.2 miles past the junction with the Broken Top trail.

Photos, left to right from top: Green Lakes Basin and South Sister; waterfall on Fall Creek; view of Broken Top from the Broken Top Trail.

TRIP PLAN

TRAILHEAD: Green Lakes

TRAILHEAD GPS COORDINATES: 44.02955, -121.73551

TRAILHEAD ELEVATION: 5,420 ft.

HIKE TYPE: basecamp with day hikes

HIKE IN TO CAMPSITES: 4.2 miles

ELEVATION GAIN: 1,200 ft.

EXPOSURE: forested and exposed

TYPICALLY OPEN: mid-July - mid-Sept.

BEST TIME: August - mid-Sept.

WATER ACCESS: streams and lakes

DOGS ALLOWED: yes, on leash only from July 15 to September 15

CAMPFIRES: not allowed in the Green Lakes area

MAPS: USGS: Broken Top; Green Trails: 622 Broken Top

FEES/PERMITS: NW Forest Pass; Backcountry permits may be required. Contact the ranger station for more info.

CONTACT

Deschutes National Forest
Bend-Fort Rock Ranger District
63095 Deschutes Market Road"
Bend, OR 97701
(541) 383-5300

Photos, left to right from top: view of Broken Top from the trail to Golden Lake; campsite near South Green Lake; wildflowers next to a stream; Green Lakes sign indicating designated campsites; Fall Creek and the Newberry Lava Flow; view of South Sister from the Green Lake trail near the pass between Broken Top and South Sister.

DAY HIKES FROM CAMP

The distance and elevation gain for each of these options is from points indicated on the map, not from the trailhead.

GREEN LAKES TO GOLDEN LAKE
6 miles round trip with 1,200 ft. gain

From the trail junction at the south end of the Green Lakes, head north on the Green Lake trail, following signs for Park Meadow. The trail passes the eastern edge of the largest Green Lake, along a slope right above the shoreline, and through a section of small rolling hills with open forest and meadows. In the summer months, this area is filled with blue lupine wildflowers. After passing Green Lake, cross through a large pumice field towards views of North Green Lake. After passing the last of the Green Lakes, the trail climbs gently towards the 7,000 ft. pass between South Sister and Broken Top.

At the pass, the terrain changes and is more open, with pink-tinged volcanic rock scattered among pumice meadows, islands of small fir and pine trees. Take in the expansive views of mountains in all directions, including Broken Top (9,175 ft.), North Sister (10,094 ft.) and Middle Sister (10,053 ft.). Continue north on the trail and look for a small side trail to the right, often marked with a cairn – a short stack of rocks placed to mark locations that may be difficult to find in rocky terrain. The 0.7 mile side trail leads to Golden Lake, with a spectacular view of nearby Broken Top.

For an extended hike, take a faint trail near the inlet creek of the lake for another mile to a set of tarns below Broken Top. Return the same way.

BROKEN TOP TRAIL
7.6 miles round trip with 880 ft. gain

At the trail junction at the south end of the Green Lakes, take the Broken Top trail to the east. Travel through rolling terrain of open forests and meadows for about two miles, crossing several small spring-fed creeks lined with wildflowers. The trail rounds an open slope below Cayuse Crater, a larger cinder cone that erupted 9,500 years ago, with views to the south of the Cascade Lakes, Diamond Peak and Mount Thielsen. At 2.8 miles, reach a trail junction with the Todd Lake Trail. Continue straight for another mile, through an open expanse of pumice fields interspersed with small meadows and ribbons of streams on the south side of Broken Top to a junction with the Crater Ditch trail. Return the same way.

For an extended hike to No Name Lake, continue past the junction with the Crater Ditch Trail, crossing Crater Creek and veer to the left onto a faint trail where the Broken Top trail turns south. Follow this rocky creek bed and scramble route as it ascends for about two miles to No Name Lake, a glacial moraine lake at the base of Broken Top. Return the same way.

DRIVING DIRECTIONS TO TRAILHEAD

From Portland, take I-5 South for 47 miles to Exit 253 for Highway 22 Detroit Lake/Bend.

At the stop light, turn left onto Highway 22.

Continue for 80 miles to a junction with Highway 20. Stay to the left and continue on Highway 20 for 25 miles to Sisters.

From Sisters, continue south on Highway 20 for 20 miles, merging onto Highway 97 / Bend Parkway South towards Mt. Bachelor/Klamath Falls.

Continue on Highway 97 South for 2.6 miles to Exit 138 for Mt. Bachelor.

Follow the Cascade Lakes National Scenic Byway / Highway 372 for 26 miles.

Turn right at a sign for the Fall Creek Trailhead.

DRIVE TIME/DISTANCE FROM PORTLAND
4 hours 20 minutes; 203 miles

ROAD CONDITIONS
Paved all the way to the trailhead.

Mount Adams Wilderness: Killen Creek

Spend a few days on Mount Adam's northwest side and hike on the Pacific Crest Trail past meadows full of wildflowers, or explore higher elevation areas via the Highline and High Camp trails.

This trip plan is based on hiking in on the Killen Creek trail and setting up a basecamp at Killen Creek. Day hike options include going north or south on the PCT, on the Highline Trail to Foggy Flat, or to High Camp, an alpine area above treeline.

THE HIKE IN

Mount Adams (12,276 ft.) is the second-highest mountain in Washington. Known as Klickitat by Native American tribes, the western portion and top of the mountain are part of the Mount Adams Wilderness, while the eastern portion is part of the Yakima Nation's territory. A potentially active stratovolcano, Mount Adams is not considered extinct, although it hasn't erupted in over 1,000 years. The Pacific Crest Trail traverses the western portion of the mountain.

Starting at the Killen Creek trailhead, the trail climbs gradually through forest for the first two miles, then travels through open meadows with views of Mount Adams for another mile. While the trail is named after Killen Creek, it's not seen until you reach the camp area to the north. The Killen Creek Trail ends at the Pacific Crest Trail (PCT), 3.1 miles from the trailhead. Turn left on the PCT and continue hiking north for just under a mile to Killen Creek. From this section of the trail, expansive views include Goat Rocks and Mount Rainier.

After crossing a small footbridge over Killen Creek, take a side trail on the left to find a campsite. Several campsites are located next to the waterfall, with more across a small meadow in a wooded area. Continuing on a faint side trail will lead to an additional camp next to a small lake. Be sure to camp in existing sites only and not on any of the fragile meadows.

Photos, left to right from top: view of Mount Adams above a bear grass-lined tarn; the PCT meanders through open meadows; sunset over an unnamed lake with Mount Rainier on the horizon.

TRIP PLAN

TRAILHEAD: Killen Creek

TRAILHEAD GPS COORDINATES: 46.28824, -121.55271

TRAILHEAD ELEVATION: 4,600 ft.

HIKE TYPE: basecamp with day hikes

HIKE IN TO CAMPSITES: 4.5 miles

ELEVATION GAIN: 1,460 ft.

EXPOSURE: mix of forest and open meadows

TYPICALLY OPEN: late-July - Sept.

BEST TIME: August

WATER ACCESS: creeks and lakes throughout the area

DOGS ALLOWED: yes

CAMPFIRES: check for current restrictions

MAPS: USGS: Green Mountain, Mount Adams West; Green Trails: Mount Adams 367S

FEES/PERMITS: NW Forest Pass; self-issued wilderness permit at the trailhead; Cascade Volcano Pass needed to explore above 7,000 ft. on the High Camp Trail

CONTACT

Gifford Pinchot National Forest
Mount Adams Ranger District
2455 Hwy 141
Trout Lake, WA 98650
(509) 395-3400

Photos, left to right from top: view of Goat Rocks from the PCT; purple asters and lupine wildflowers; campsite at Killen Creek; waterfall on Killen Creek; hiking in on the Killen Creek trail.

MOUNT ADAMS WILDERNESS: KILLEN CREEK

DAY HIKES FROM CAMP

The distance and elevation gain for each of these options is from points indicated on the map, not from the trailhead.

FOGGY FLAT
5.5 miles round trip, 700 ft. gain

From the Killen Creek camp area, head north on the PCT for about a quarter of a mile to the junction with the Highline Trail. Stay to the right and take the Highline Trail as it heads east on the north side of Mount Adams. The trail doesn't gain much elevation, but it does undulate up and down over the terrain all the way to Foggy Flat – a relatively flat, large, open meadow on the north side of Mount Adams. On the way there, the trail passes through many small meadows filled with wildflowers and provides big views of Mount Adams and the Lyman and Lava glaciers. Explore the area around Foggy Flat before returning to camp.

Continuing on the Highline Trail past Foggy Flat requires crossing two potentially difficult glacial branches of the Muddy Fork.

HIGH CAMP & SOUTH ON THE PCT
6.5 miles round trip, 1,000 ft. gain

From the Killen Creek camp area, head south on the PCT. Continue a short distance past the junction with the Killen Creek Trail and look for a trail junction with the High Camp Trail. Turn left and head up this trail through open rocky areas, with wide-horizon views of Mount Rainier and Goat Rocks to the north. The terrain gets rockier the higher up you go, eventually leaving treeline as the trail crosses steep talus slopes before arriving at an alpine camp area at the base of Mount Adams' bulky mass.

To continue the hike, return on the High Camp Trail to the junction with the PCT. Turn left and head south on the PCT, passing several seasonal tarns and meadows filled with wildflowers. After rounding a rocky ridge with bear grass lining the trail, look for views of Mount St. Helens on the horizon. The end point of this section is Adams Creek – a fast moving glacier-fed creek that can be difficult to cross. Turn around and follow the PCT north for 2.3 miles back to camp at Killen Creek.

DRIVING DIRECTIONS TO TRAILHEAD

From Portland, drive east on I-84 for 61 miles to Exit 64 / Hood River / Highway 35.

Turn left and cross the Columbia River on the Hood River bridge ($2 toll).

At Highway 14, turn left and continue west for 1.5 miles to Highway 141 Alt.

Turn right onto Highway 141 Alt, merging onto Highway 141 after two miles.

Continue on Highway 141, heading towards Trout Lake for another 19 miles.

Make a slight right turn onto Mount Adams Road.

Continue for 1.3 miles to a junction with Buck Creek Road / NF-23 / Randle Road.

Make a slight left turn onto NF-23 and continue for 23.2 miles to NF-2329.

Make a slight right turn onto NF-2329, staying to the right at 1.2 miles.

Continue on NF-2329 for 4.6 miles to the Killen Creek trailhead.

DRIVE TIME/DISTANCE FROM PORTLAND

2 hours 30 minutes; 118 miles

ROAD CONDITIONS

The last 9 miles are gravel, suitable for most vehicles.

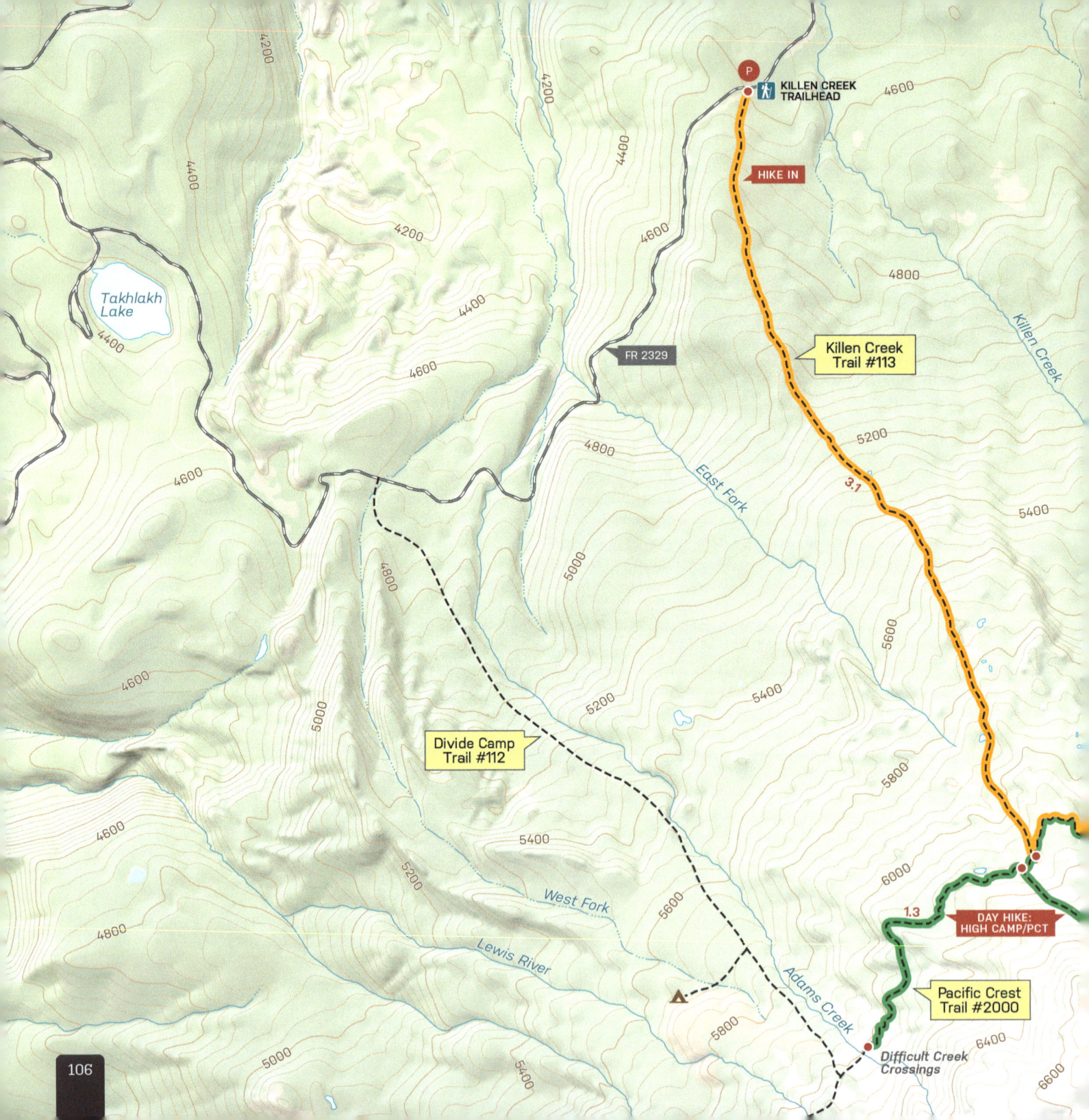

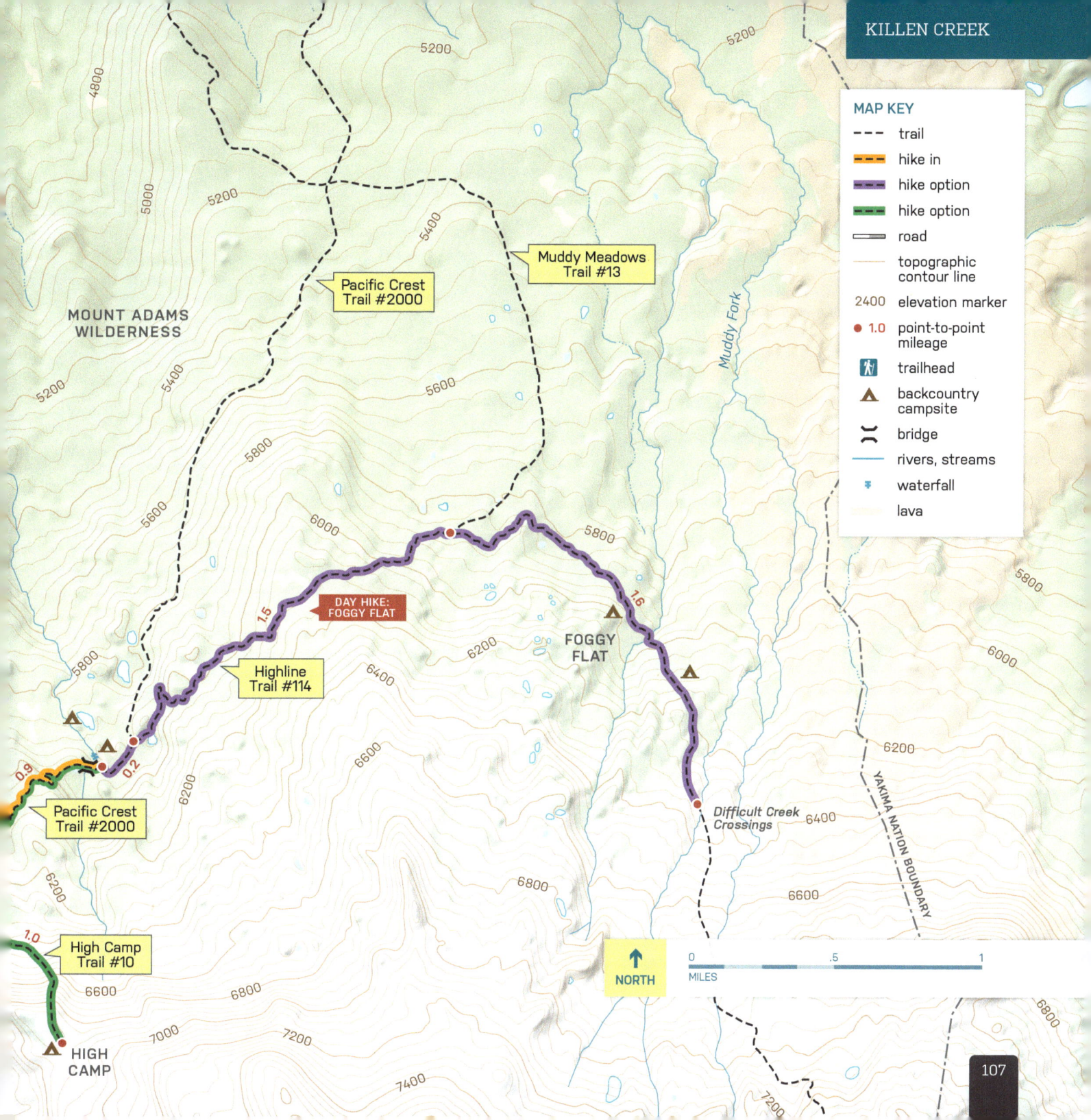

Mount Hood Wilderness: Cairn Basin

Cairn Basin provides access to the northwest side of Mount Hood's subalpine meadows — with meandering streams and panoramic views of surrounding ridges.

This trip plan is based on setting up basecamp at an established campsite in Cairn Basin, with day hike options to McNeil Point, Wy'East Basin and Elk Cove.

THE HIKE IN

Beginning at the Top Spur trailhead, head up the root-filled trail for 0.5 miles to a junction with the Pacific Crest Trail (PCT). Turn right on the PCT and continue for just over 250 feet to a large junction with the Timberline Trail (a 40 mile route that circumnavigates the mountain) and a wilderness permit station. Fill out a permit and decide which of two trail options to consider: while the Timberline Trail (Cairn Basin) is a more direct route to Cairn Basin, the Timberline Trail (Muddy Fork) route loops around Bald Mountain with expansive views and adds just under a half-mile to the hike. A third trail on the right is where the PCT heads steeply downhill to the Muddy Fork of the Sandy River. For the recommended scenic route, take the Timberline Trail (Muddy Fork) — to the right of the wilderness permit station — and head around the face of Bald Mountain. After a short trek in the forest, the trail opens to outstanding views of Mount Hood, Yocum Ridge, and the valley of the Muddy Fork of the Sandy River far below.

After 0.9 miles on this trail, look to the left for the Cutoff Trail junction and hike over a small saddle to return to the Timberline Trail (Cairn Basin). Turn right and continue uphill through a cathedral forest of Douglas fir, noble fir, and mountain hemlock with an understory of huckleberries that ripen in August. Head up Bald Mountain Ridge, then pass through two open meadow areas on the side of the ridge with stunning views of Mount Hood.

Continue on the trail through a steep forested section with several switchbacks, and cross a couple of cascading streams before entering a scenic area with meadows. In July and August, wildflowers may include red paintbrush, blue lupine, avalanche lilies, western pasqueflower, beargrass, heather, and pink spiraea. Pass a large scree slope and several tarns (ponds created by snow melt), then continue to the right and uphill on the Timberline Trail towards Cairn Basin. At 4.2 miles, pass the junction with the Mazama Trail, and after another 0.3 miles, pass the junction with the McNeil Point trail.

Panoramic views to the north include Mount St. Helens, Mount Rainier and Mount Adams. Continue on the Timberline Trail, rock hopping across silt-filled Ladd Creek. After crossing the creek, continue for another 0.2 miles to Cairn Basin. This area was significantly burned in the 2011 Dollar Lake Fire, leaving sections of the forest with black and white snags. Cairn Basin shelter, one of three remaining stone shelters on Mount Hood that were built in the 1930s by the Civilian Conservation Corps, survived the fire. Several side trails lead to numerous campsites in this area, with a tributary of Ladd Creek on the northern end of Cairn Basin. Small meadows behind the camp area are great for catching glimpses of alpenglow on the mountain at sunset.

Photos, left to right from top: hiking into Cairn Basin; tarns on the Timberline Trail; Ladd Creek.

TRIP PLAN

TRAILHEAD: Top Spur

TRAILHEAD GPS COORDINATES: 45.4074, -121.7856

TRAILHEAD ELEVATION: 3,900 ft.

HIKE TYPE: basecamp with day hikes

HIKE IN TO CAMPSITES: 4.6 miles

ELEVATION GAIN: 2,200 ft.

EXPOSURE: mix of forest and open meadows

TYPICALLY OPEN: mid-July - Oct.

BEST TIME: August - Sept.

WATER ACCESS: streams

DOGS ALLOWED: yes

CAMPFIRES: check for current restrictions

MAPS: USGS: Bull Run Lake, Mount Hood North; Green Trails: Mount Hood 462S

FEES/PERMITS: NW Forest Pass, self-issued wilderness permit at the trailhead

CONTACT

Mount Hood National Forest
Zigzag Ranger Station
70220 E Highway 26
Zigzag, Oregon 97049
(503) 622-3191

Photos, left to right from top: small rock walls provide shelter for tents on the ridge above McNeil Point; Timberline Trail forest; McNeil Point shelter; campsite at Cairn Basin; trail around Bald Mountain; expansive view from McNeil Point.

MOUNT HOOD WILDERNSS: CAIRN BASIN

DAY HIKES FROM CAMP

The distance and elevation gain for each of these options is from points indicated on the map, not from the trailhead.

MCNEIL POINT
3 miles round trip, 1,000 ft. gain (from Cairn Basin camp area)

Conditions on this high exposed area can change quickly, so be prepared with warm layers of clothing and rain gear. A good general rule is that if the mountain is completely socked in, it's best to do this hike another day. It's easy to get lost in high mountain terrain, and the effort to get there is better rewarded when there are views all around.

From camp, head back on the Timberline trail for 0.2 miles to the McNeil Point trail junction. Turn left and follow the McNeil Point Trail on a ridge above Ladd Creek. Stay right at all junctions, hiking through forest, past rock slides and up a ridge beside Ladd Creek. At times, the trail is hard to distinguish as it goes through thick shrubbery. Snowfields can linger on the rocky slopes all year. Continue up a steep ridge and stay to the right to the McNeil Point stone shelter, built in the 1930s by the Civilian Conservation Corps.

Take in amazing views in all directions, including Mount Rainier, Mount St. Helens and Mount Adams on the horizon to the north. After soaking in this glorious high mountain region, return the same way back to camp.

Going farther: For a closer look at the Sandy and Glisan glaciers, continue on the trail above the shelter.

WY'EAST BASIN + ELK COVE
5.3 miles round trip, 1,300 ft. gain (from Cairn Basin camp area)

From camp, head northeast on the Timberline Trail. If water levels are low enough, rock hop across a tributary of Ladd Creek, then head uphill to the junction with the Vista Ridge Trail, just over a mile from Cairn Basin's camp area. Turn right to stay on the Timberline Trail and pass through Wy'East Basin's meadows, with expansive views to the north.

Reach a junction with the Pinnacle Ridge Trail and after another 0.3 miles, look for a small cairn marking a sidepath to Dollar Lake. This short 0.2 mile trail leads to tiny Dollar Lake, with a couple of campsites near the lake and just above it. Barrett Spur looms large above Dollar Lake, with the rugged northwest face of Mount Hood directly behind it.

Head back to the Timberline Trail and turn right to go to Elk Cove. The trail turns and descends alongside cliffs and talus slopes with views of the meadows below. Cross a small creek lined with wildflowers in July and August, and reach a junction with the Elk Cove Trail. Camping is not allowed in the meadows, but there are several campsites in the forest a short distance north on the Elk Cove Trail. Head back to camp the same way.

DRIVING DIRECTIONS TO TRAILHEAD
From Portland: drive 42 miles east on U.S. 26 to Zigzag.

Across from the Zigzag Ranger District, turn left onto East Lolo Pass Road.

Continue for 4.2 miles, then fork right on paved road 1825.

After 0.7 miles, just before a bridge over the Sandy River, go straight on Road 1828 (paved single lane road with turnouts).

Continue 5.6 miles and fork to the right on gravel Road 118 for 1.5 miles to the Top Spur Trailhead.

DRIVE TIME/DISTANCE FROM PORTLAND
1 hour 40 minutes; 52 miles

ROAD CONDITIONS
Final 1.5 miles are gravel with potholes, suitable for most vehicles.

Mount Hood Wilderness: Burnt Lake

The alpenglow on Mount Hood reflected in Burnt Lake is a sight you won't soon forget. Take this moderately easy hike to a mountain lake and stay overnight to watch the mountain change colors several times in a day.

This trip plan is based on setting up basecamp at an established campsite at Burnt Lake, with day hikes to East Zigzag Mountain and Cast Lake.

THE HIKE IN

From the trailhead, go through a wood stile designed to keep horses and bicycles off the trail. For the first two miles, the trail is relatively flat and gentle as it heads through a forest of Douglas fir, hemlock and old-growth cedar that burned in 1904 and 1906, which is how Burnt Lake got its name. The forest has since filled in, while many hollow shells of burnt old-growth cedars remain. At 2.5 miles, take a side trail that leads a short distance down to views of Lost Creek Falls. Back on the main trail, after a sharp turn, the path climbs more steeply on the final mile to Burnt Lake. As you make your way up the switchbacks on the trail, look for views of Mount Hood. Rock hop across the lake's outlet stream, and in another .25 mile, reach the shores of 8-acre Burnt Lake.

Side trails lead to either campsites or day-use areas. Set up camp away from the lake in one of seven designated campsites – each marked with a wooden post. Sites #1, #2 and #3 are above the northwest side of the lake. Site #1 is accessed via the first side trail before you reach the lake. To reach sites #2-3, continue to a trail junction and take the main Burnt Lake Trail as it heads up the ridge, leaving the lake. To access sites #4-7, take the first side trail to the left and follow the faint path to the north side of the lake. Boardwalks take you over the lake's outlet, then the first of several campsites will be behind the trees next to the lake. Campfires are not allowed within 1/2 mile of Burnt Lake. If you want to explore around the camp area, a faint and brushy trail goes all the way around the lake.

This is a popular area than can get crowded, especially in the summer. To avoid crowds, arrive mid-week or early on a Friday morning for a weekend trip. If there are no campsites, or for more seclusion, continue for 2.4 additional miles to Cast Lake (see the map).

For views of Mount Hood, especially nice at sunrise and sunset, head to day-use area D on the southwest side of Burnt Lake and make your way through the overgrown path to the lake shore. On clear nights, this is a great place to see the sky full of stars.

Photos, left to right from top: Burnt Lake and Mount Hood; forest on the hike in; trail to the summit of East Zigzag Mountain.

TRIP PLAN

TRAILHEAD: Burnt Lake North

TRAILHEAD GPS COORDINATES: 45.3720, -121.8225

TRAILHEAD ELEVATION: 2,665 ft.

HIKE TYPE: basecamp with day hikes

HIKE IN TO CAMPSITES: 3.5 miles

ELEVATION GAIN: 1,500 ft

EXPOSURE: forested

TYPICALLY OPEN: June - October

BEST TIME: August - early Oct.

WATER ACCESS: Burnt Lake

DOGS ALLOWED: Yes

CAMPFIRES: Not allowed within 1/2 mile of Burnt Lake

MAPS: USGS: Government Camp; Green Trails: Government Camp

FEES/PERMITS: NW Forest Pass, self-issued wilderness permit at the trailhead

CONTACT

Mount Hood National Forest
Zigzag Ranger Station
70220 E Highway 26
Zigzag, Oregon 97049
(503) 622-3191

Photos, left to right from top: Burnt Lake and Mount Hood at sunrise; at the summit of East Zigzag Mountain; campsite at Burnt Lake; heading up to East Zigzag Mountain; one of many hollowed-out cedars on the hike in; view of Mount Hood and Burnt Lake from the ridge of East Zigzag.

DAY HIKES FROM CAMP

The distance and elevation gain for each of these options is from points indicated on the map, not from the trailhead.

EAST ZIGZAG MOUNTAIN
2.6 miles round trip, 800 ft. gain (from Burnt Lake)

From Burnt Lake, continue on the Burnt Lake Trail as it heads up a ridge away from the lake for 0.8 mile, passing campsites #2 and #3. Continue on this trail past a boggy section, then up several switchbacks to a saddle and a junction with the Zigzag Mountain Trail #775. Turn right and head up a short, steep and rocky trail. Rhododendrons line the trail at an opening on the ridge with views of Mount Hood and Burnt Lake, now far below. Continue on the ridge for 0.3 mile to an open saddle and pass a junction with the Burnt Lake South Trail. The steep slope of East Zigzag Mountain is directly ahead. Continue up this open ridge on a rocky path for another 0.2 mile, past stands of conifers and shrubs to the rocky summit of East Zigzag Mountain (4,971 ft.). A fire lookout used to be here, but now there's nothing but a jumble of boulders and rock. Make your way across the rocks and find a spot to relax and soak in the massive views of five volcanoes. Mount Hood looms large directly to the west, and on clear days, Mount St. Helens, Mount Rainier and Mount Adams can be seen on the horizon looking north, while Mount Jefferson is viewed to the south through an opening in trees.

CAST LAKE
4.8 miles round trip, 1,300 ft. gain (from Burnt Lake)

Follow the directions above to East Zigzag Mountain, then continue west past the summit for 0.5 mile to a junction with the Cast Creek Trail #773. Turn left and continue for 0.1 mile and the Cast Lake Trail #796. Turn right and follow this trail, climbing slightly before dropping down to the lake in 0.5 mile. While there are no big views at Cast Lake, there are a couple of campsites on the north and south sides of this small and secluded lake.

DRIVING DIRECTIONS TO TRAILHEAD

From Portland: drive 42 miles east on U.S. 26 to Zigzag.

Across from the Zigzag Ranger District, turn left onto East Lolo Pass Road.

Continue on Lolo Pass Road for 4.2 miles, then turn right on paved Forest Road 1825.

Drive for 0.7 miles on Forest Road 1825 and turn right to cross the Sandy River on a bridge.

Continue for another 1.7 miles and bear right at the junction onto Forest Road 1825-109.

Continue for 1.4 miles on this gravel road to the trailhead parking lot.

DRIVE TIME/DISTANCE FROM PORTLAND
1 hour 30 minutes; 50 miles

ROAD CONDITIONS
There are a few potholes on the last 1.4 miles of gravel road, but it's suitable for most vehicles.

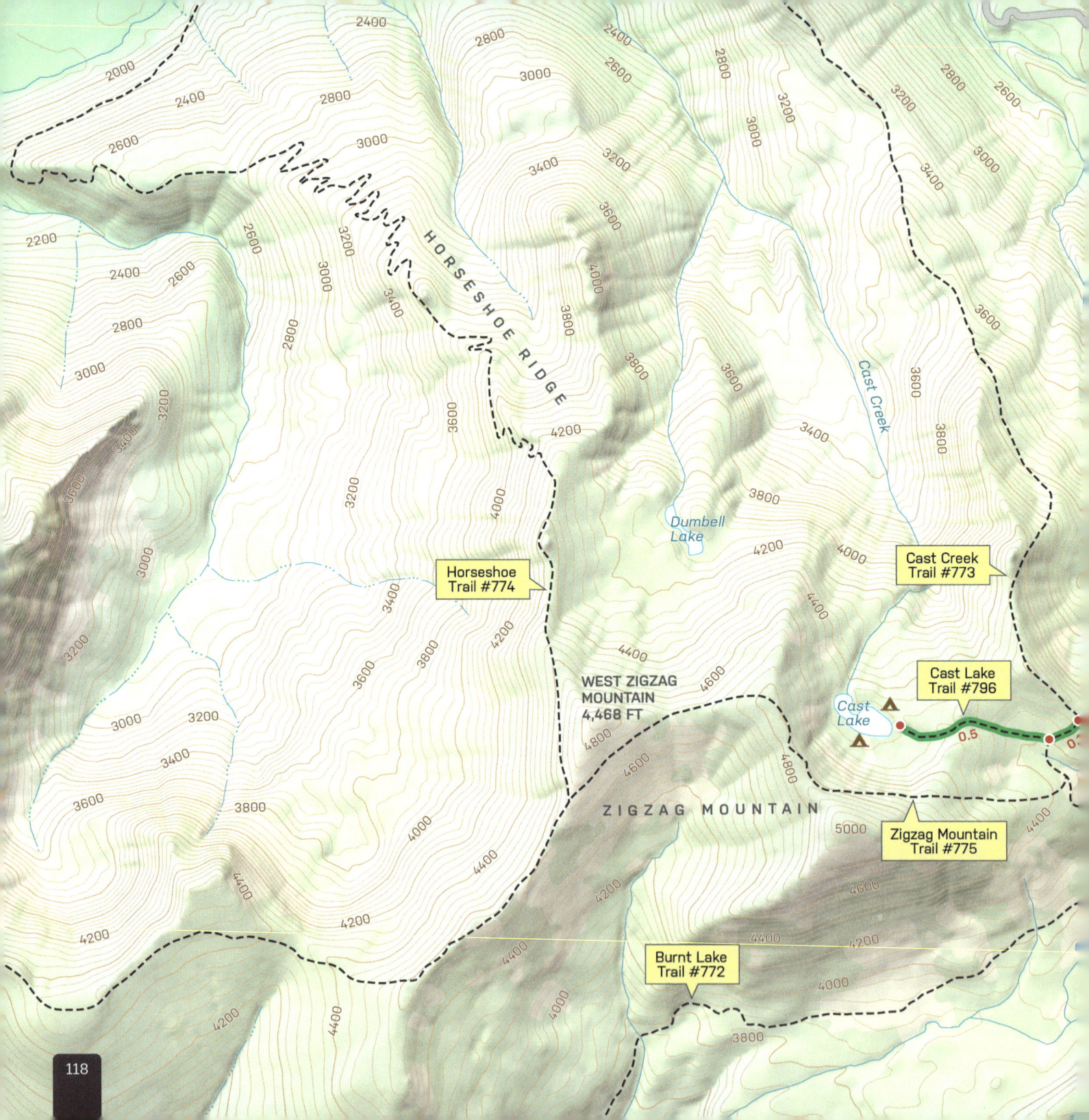

Indian Heaven Wilderness: Deep Lake

Late autumn is the best time of year to visit Indian Heaven Wilderness. The mosquitoes the area is famous for are gone, and thousands of huckleberry-laden shrubs literally cover the entire area in stunning shades of red, yellow and orange.

This trip planned is based on camping at Deep Lake. However, there are campsites at many of the lakes in this area, so if the few campsites at Deep Lake fill up, just head to another lake.

THE HIKE IN

Indian Heaven Wilderness is a special place. Native American tribes gathered here annually for almost 10,000 years to gather the plentiful huckleberries, fish in the 150+ small lakes that dot the region, hunt, trade, race horses, and celebrate together. Through a rare handshake agreement in 1932 by the Yakima Nation and the Forest Service, the Sawtooth Berry Fields on the north end of the wilderness were designated for exclusive use by local tribes.

The area is generally snow free by mid-July, but the swarms of mosquitos in the summer make this area known as "mosquito heaven," so it's best to wait until at least late August to visit. For the best fall color, visit in mid-to-late September.

This hike begins at the south end of the Cultus Creek campground near a sign for "Indian Heaven Trail No. 33." The trail is steep right away, climbing 1,200 feet in about 1.5 miles. At just over one mile in, pass through a rocky section with views to the north and east, including an up-front view of Mount Adams with Goat Rocks and Mount Rainier on the horizon. The trail levels out near the base of Bird Mountain and goes through several sections of forest and open meadow before reaching a side trail to Deep Lake at 2.2 miles in.

Take the short side trail for 0.2 mile to Deep Lake. The trail splits to head around the lake in both directions. The best campsites are about halfway around the lake on the north and south. One or two additional but much smaller campsites can be found nearby.

A faint trail goes all the way around the lake, but it's overgrown in a few spots and easy to lose among many user paths. Just stay close the lake whenever there is an option. The tip of Mount Adams can be seen from the southwest side of Deep Lake, and continuing around the southern shore, the ridge in view immediately to the west is Bird Mountain.

Additional campsites are located at Cultus Lake, Lemei Lake, Bear Lake, Elk Lake, Deer Lake, Junction Lake, and Clear Lake.

Photos, left to right from top: Cultus Lake; side trail to Deep Lake; Deep Lake

---

TRIP PLAN

TRAILHEAD: Indian Heaven Trail #33

TRAILHEAD GPS COORDINATES: 46.0470, -121.7563

TRAILHEAD ELEVATION: 4,000 ft.

HIKE TYPE: basecamp with day hikes

HIKE IN TO CAMPSITES: 2.2 miles

ELEVATION GAIN: 1,200 ft.

EXPOSURE: mix of forest and open meadows

TYPICALLY OPEN: July - October

BEST TIME: mid-Sept. - early October

WATER ACCESS: at any of the lakes

DOGS ALLOWED: yes

CAMPFIRES: check for current restrictions

MAPS: Green Trails: Indian Heaven 365S

FEES/PERMITS: NW Forest Pass; self-issued wilderness permit at the trailhead

CONTACT

Gifford Pinchot National Forest
Mt. Adams Ranger District
2455 Hwy 141
Trout Lake, WA 98650
(509) 395-3400

Photos, left to right from top: Lemei Lake; meadows with huckleberries; Lake Wapiki; Junction Lake; Bear Lake as seen from the Pacific Crest Trail; Lemei Rock.

DAY HIKES FROM CAMP

The distance and elevation gain for each of these options is from points indicated on the map, not from the trailhead.

LEMEI ROCK
4 miles round trip, 800 ft. gain (from Deep Lake)

From camp at Deep Lake, head back to the Indian Heaven Trail #33 and turn left to head south on the trail. A short distance ahead (0.2 mile), turn left at the junction with the Lemei Trail #34. Pass through open meadows filled with huckleberry shrubs and heather. **Lemei Rock** (5,925 ft.) comes into view long before you reach it. An ancient shield volcano, Lemei Rock is the highest point in Indian Heaven. Lemei is pronounced "Lem-ee-eye" and is Chinook jargon for "old woman." Just before reaching Lemei Rock, enter a wooded section with trail switchbacks. Along this section of the trail, look through the trees to the west for a glimpse of Mount St. Helens. Leave the woods and follow the side of a small talus slope. Look to the north for views of ridge after ridge, with Mount Rainier on the horizon. A short distance later, note a faint side trail to explore more around the base of Lemei Rock. However, for expansive views, continue for about 0.25 mile to a red cinder rim overlooking Lake Wapiki and continue across this ridge to a viewpoint. Mount Adams dominates the view to the northeast, with Mount Hood to the south. Return to camp the same way.

For further exploration, and to reach Lake Wapiki, continue past the viewpoint for about 0.5 mile on a steep descent to a junction with the Wapiki Trail. Take this trail for another 0.4 mile to Lake Wapiki.

LAKES BASIN LOOP
6.5 miles round trip, 900 ft. gain (from Deep Lake)

From camp at Deep Lake, take the side trail back to the Indian Heaven Trail #33 and turn left to head south. Continue to a junction with the Lemei Lake Trail #179 (not to be confused with the Lemei Trail #34). Turn right and take the Lemei Trail through grassy meadows filled with huckleberry shrubs for 0.6 mile to the scenic outlet of Lemei Lake. Pass side trails that lead to campsites, then continue up switchbacks in a forested section before heading back through meadow after meadow of subalpine beauty. Just before reaching Junction Lake, the trail begins a gentle descent through the forest, then leaves the woods and travels along the shore of shallow Junction Lake. Small campsites are located via faint side trails on either side of the lake. East Crater, a shield volcano, sits above the lake. A lightning-caused wildfire in 2017 partially burned the slopes of East Crater.

The Lemei Lake Trail ends at a junction with the Pacific Crest Trail #2000 (PCT). Turn right and head north on the PCT. The next section of this loop is mainly forested, with fewer huckleberry shrubs or meadows. After 1 mile on the PCT, Bear Lake can be seen to the left and through the trees. The Elk Lake #176 side trail leads to camps at Bear Lake and to secluded Elk Lake. Continue on the PCT and pass Deer Lake on the left, then reach a junction with the Indian Heaven Trail #33. Turn right and the trail begins an easy ascent, passing a large talus slope near Clear Lake. Pikas can often be heard "meeping" in the rocky talus. Side trails near the shore of Clear Lake lead to more campsites. Continue past the Lemei Lake and Lemei Trail junctions on the way back to the Deep Lake Trail and camp.

DRIVING DIRECTIONS TO TRAILHEAD

From Portland, drive east on I-84 for 62 miles to Hood River.

Take Exit 64 and turn left.

Cross the Hood River Bridge over the Columbia River ($2 toll).

Turn left onto Highway 14 and continue for 1.5 miles.

Turn right onto WA-141 Alternative and continue for 2.2 miles.

Turn left onto WA-141 and continue for 19 miles.

In the town of Trout Lake, make a slight left to stay on WA-141.

Continue for 5.9 miles to the forest boundary, where WA-141 becomes Forest Road 24.

Continue on Forest Road 24 for 2.4 miles to the intersection with Forest Road 60. At the intersection turn right to stay on Forest Road 24 and continue north for 9 miles to Cultus Creek Campground.

Park at the south end of the campground by a sign for Indian Heaven Trail 33.

DRIVE TIME/DISTANCE FROM PORTLAND
2 hours 20 minutes; 105 miles

ROAD CONDITIONS
Gravel road for the last 9 miles, suitable for most vehicles.

Index

A
About the authors 4
Abrasions 51

B
Backpack, how to pack 48
Backpacking gear 8
Backpacking styles 32
Backpacking tents 12
Backpacks (gear) 10
Bathroom kit 25
Bathroom, using in the backcountry 58
Battery backup devices 26
Bear bags 19
Bear canisters 19
Bears 46
Bidet (gear) 25
Bidet (using) 59
Blisters 50
Boiling water for purification 21
Burns 51

C
Cameras 26
Campfires 60
Camp kitchens 54
Campsite selection 52
Chairs 27
Chemical treatment for water purification 21
Clothing 22
Compass 47
Conditions, current 37
Cookware 19
Courtesies, trail 45

D
Dental hygiene 25
Documentation 35

E
Electronic navigation 47
Electronics 26
Emergency planning 38
Emergency shelter (ten essentials) 29

F
Filtering water 56
Fire starter (ten essentials) 29
First aid basics 50
First-aid (ten essentials) 29
Food, clean up 54
Food for backpacking 57
Food preparation 54
Food sacks 19
Food storage 19, 54
Footwear 24

G
Gear 8
    Backpacking chairs 27
    Backpacking tents 12
    Backpacks 10
    Clothing 22
    Electronics 26
    Footwear 24
    Kitchen 18
    Sleep systems 15
    Ten Essentials 29
    Toiletries 25
    Trekking poles 27
    Water storage 21
    Water Treatment 20
Gear maintenance 62
Giving forward 63
Gravity systems for water filtering 20
Groups, planning for 35

H
Hanging food 54
Heat-related illness 51
Hiking safety 44
Hydration bladders 21
Hygiene, personal 59
Hypothermia 51

I
Illumination (ten essentials) 29
Insects 37
Insulation (ten essentials) 29
Itinerary 39

K
Kitchen gear 18
Kitchens, camp 54

L
Land managers 33
Layering 22
Leave No Trace Seven Principles 40
Lightweight backpacking 9

M
Maps, preparing 34
Menstruation products, using 59
Menstruation supplies 25

N
Navigation 47
Navigation (ten essentials) 29
Non-profit organizations 63

O
Odor-proof bags 19

P

Packing a backpack 48
Passes 34
PCT food hang method 55
Peeing in the backcountry 58
Permits 34
Personal hygiene 59
Pets 46
Physical preparation 42
Pillows 17
Pooping in the backcountry 58
Pumps for filtering water 21
Putting a pack on 49

Q

Quilts 15

R

Ranger stations 33
Regulations 34
Repair kit (ten essentials) 29

S

Safety & Emergency Planning 38
Safety, hiking 44
Skills 30
Sleeping bags 15
Sleeping pads 17
Sleep systems 15
Smartphones 26
Socks 24
SOS devices 26
Squeeze filters 20
Staying warm 61
Stewardship 63
Stoves 18
Stream crossings 45
Stretches 43
Sun protection 29

T

Ten essentials 29
Tents 12
Tides 38
Toilet paper 58
Toiletries 25
Toilets in the backcountry 59
Trail courtesies 45
Trekking poles 27
Trip itinerary 39
Trip planning basics 31
Trip prep 36
Trips 64
    Columbia River Gorge, Wahtum Lake 79
    Eagle Cap Wilderness, Wallowas Lakes Basin 85
    Goat Rocks Wilderness, Snowgrass Flat 91
    Indian Heaven Wilderness, Deep Lake 121
    Mount Adams Wilderness, Killen Creek 103
    Mount Hood Wilderness, Burnt Lake 115
    Mount Hood Wilderness, Cairn Basin 109
    Oregon Coast, Tillamook Head 73
    Southwest Washington, Siouxon Creek 67
    Three Sisters Wilderness, Green Lakes 97
Trowel 25

U

UV water purifiers 21

W

Waste, packing out general 53
Waste, packing out toilet 59
Water, filtering 56
Water filters (gear) 20
Water storage (gear) 21
Weather forecasts 37
Weather, hiking safety 37, 44
Wildfires 37
Wildlife 46

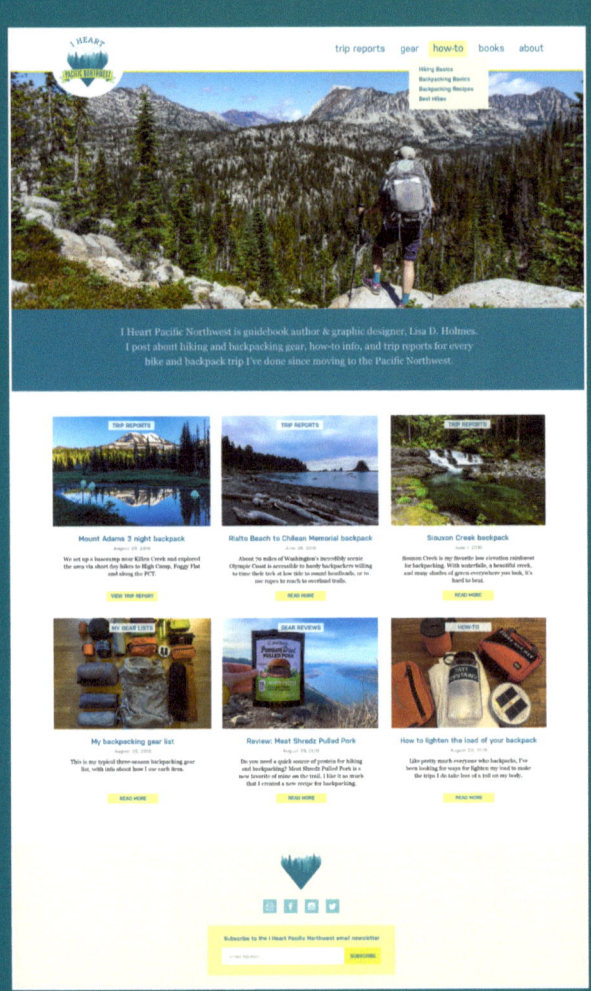

The **I Heart Pacific Northwest** website is a companion guide to this book, featuring a detailed list of recommended backpacking gear, trip reports, gear reviews, and how-to info.

iheartpacificnorthwest.com